Praise for *Sigil Witchery*

"In *Sigil Witchery*, Laura Tempest Zakroff—a powerful Witch, a gift offers that rarest of magical hen's teeth: a highly original, powerful new way to work magic. Most books on magic and Witchcraft rehash the same old methods and techniques over and over with no more than minor variations. To the best of my own knowledge, Tempest has invented an entire new approach to making and using sigils here, and I think it is an extremely powerful one ... I recommend this book in the highest possible terms."

—Robert Mathiesen, Professor Emeritus, Brown University, and co-author of *The Rede of the Wiccae*

"This wonderful book takes the concept of sigil well beyond the simplistic, basic notions of the [Austin Osman] Spare method, and opens the door on the deeper art and potential of sigils as it applies across the spectrum of spellcraft. Any student of the occult with an interest in sigils and sigil crafting: this is a book you need."

—Arjil, teacher of Just Effing Magick and creator of the Ellis Sigil

"With style, wisdom, and a generous dose of humor, artist and author Laura Tempest Zakroff offers us a new look at an ancient magical practice: the creation and use of sigils, as well as modern tools to take this practice to the next level. From the historical and ritual use of symbols, signs, seals, and marks to the creative process itself, including tools and artistic techniques, *Sigil Witchery* makes an impressive contribution to a traditional body of occult knowledge."

—Storm Faerywolf, author of *Betwixt and Between* and *The Stars Within the Earth*

"*Sigil Witchery* pulls together a number of threads in contemporary magic with insight and intelligence while keeping the applications of magical symbolism front and center. Zakroff's study ranges from the tattoo patterns of the Amazigh people to graffiti tags found in urban alleys, yet the wide scope of her interests never gets in the way of her clear writing. Her approach to sigil craft is rooted, practical, imaginative, and inspiring."

—Cory Thomas Hutcheson, author and co-host of *New World Witchery*

"Full of original art, sigils, massive research, and a clear writing and teaching style, this is definitely the best book on the subject of sigils that has ever been written, hands down. This book isn't just a showcase of historical sigil methods or rehashed information. Tempest brings new creative ideas to the table while placing a focus on directly interacting with the book's material to make sigil magick your very own personalized form of witchery."

—Mat Auryn, professional psychic, witch, writer, and blogger at Patheos Pagan

"*Sigil Witchery* perfectly combines the history and art of mark-making with the science and art of magick."

—Chris Orapello, author, artist, and co-host of *Down at the Crossroads*

"With this book, Tempest totally shifts the idea of using magical sigils from a rote, rather dry process to an artistic creation that you don't have to be a gifted artist to do. She brings this information in a conversational way; it's easy to follow, fun, and full of historical details with a modern perspective … After reading it I felt super inspired to create a sigil and have it tattooed on me!"

—Phoenix LeFae, author of *Hoodoo Shrines and Altars*

"*Sigil Witchery* delves into areas of sigil work not commonly discussed. Additionally, it provides the reader with all the tools needed to enrich their practice with the power, magic, and wisdom that comes from crafting personalized magical symbols. Highly recommend to anyone interested in the intersection of art, magic, and symbol."

—Matthew Venus, artist, sigilic magician, and magical apothecary

ABOUT THE AUTHOR

Laura Tempest Zakroff is a professional artist, author, dancer, designer, muse, mythpunk, teacher, and Witch. She holds a BFA from the Rhode Island School of Design and her artwork has received awards and honors worldwide. Laura has been a practicing Modern Traditional Witch for over two decades and revels in the intersection of her various paths with Witchcraft. She blogs for Patheos as *A Modern Traditional Witch* and for Witches & Pagans as *Fine Art Witchery* and contributes to *The Witches' Almanac*, *Llewellyn's Magical Almanac*, and *Llewellyn's Witches' Companion*. *Sigil Witchery* is her second book, her first being *The Witch's Cauldron*, released in 2017. Laura resides in Seattle, Washington, with her partner, Nathaniel Johnstone, and at least three cats. Find out more at www. lauratempestzakroff.com.

A
WITCH'S GUIDE TO CRAFTING
MAGICK SYMBOLS

Sigil Witchery

LAURA TEMPEST ZAKROFF

Llewellyn Publications
Woodbury, Minnesota

First Edition
Sixth Printing, 2021

Book design by Donna Burch-Brown
Cover design by Ellen Lawson
Interior art and photos by Laura Tempest Zakroff, except for the photo on page 107 by Kohenet Ketzirah haMa'agelet and the photo on page 126 by Carrie Meyer

Llewellyn Publications is a registered trademark of Llewellyn Worldwide Ltd.

Library of Congress Cataloging-in-Publication Data
Names: Tempest Zakroff, Laura, author.
Title: Sigil witchery : a witch's guide to crafting magick symbols / by Laura
    Tempest Zakroff.
Description: First Edition. | Woodbury : Llewellyn Worldwide, Ltd., 2018. |
    Includes bibliographical references and index.
Identifiers: LCCN 2017043218 (print) | LCCN 2017045801 (ebook) | ISBN
    9780738755854 () | ISBN 9780738753690
Subjects: LCSH: Sigils. | Magic. | Witchcraft.
Classification: LCC BF1623.S5 (ebook) | LCC BF1623.S5 T46 2018 (print) | DDC
    133.4/3—dc23
LC record available at https://lccn.loc.gov/2017043218

Llewellyn Worldwide Ltd. does not participate in, endorse, or have any authority or responsibility concerning private business transactions between our authors and the public.
    All mail addressed to the author is forwarded but the publisher cannot, unless specifically instructed by the author, give out an address or phone number.
    Any internet references contained in this work are current at publication time, but the publisher cannot guarantee that a specific location will continue to be maintained. Please refer to the publisher's website for links to authors' websites and other sources.

Llewellyn Publications
A Division of Llewellyn Worldwide Ltd.
2143 Wooddale Drive
Woodbury, MN 55125-2989
www.llewellyn.com

Printed in the United States of America

Other Books by Laura Tempest Zakroff

The Witch's Cauldron:
The Craft, Lore & Magick of Ritual Vessels
(Llewellyn, 2017)

Forthcoming Books by Laura Tempest Zakroff

The Witch's Altar:
The Craft, Lore & Magick of Shrines
(with Jason Mankey, Llewellyn, 2018)

Weave the Liminal:
The Path of the Modern Traditional Witch
(Llewellyn, 2019)

Other Works by Laura Tempest Zakroff

Coloring Books

Steampunk Menagerie
(2015)

Myth & Magick
(2016)

The Art of Bellydance
(2016)

Witch's Brew
(2016)

Instructional DVDs

Bellydance Artistry

(2011)

DecoDance

(2015)

Contributions

Llewellyn's 2019 Magical Almanac

(Contributing author, Llewellyn, 2019)

Llewellyn's 2019 Witches' Companion

(Contributing author, Llewellyn, 2019)

The Witches' Almanac, Spring 2017–2018, 2018–2019

(Contributing author, The Witches' Almanac, LTD)

Witches & Pagans and *SageWoman* magazines

(Illustrator, BBI Media)

The Witch's Book of Shadows by Jason Mankey

(Contributing author, Llewellyn, 2017)

For my parents, Pete and Terry Zakroff.
Thank you for believing in your crazy artist daughter.
From putting up with 10-foot-tall chicken-wire/plaster-wrap goddesses,
salt block sculptures, and life-size horses painted on my bedroom walls
to collecting my latest creations and commissioning me to paint your mailbox,
your support for my work throughout my entire life has made all the difference.

Contents

Illustrations and Photographs . . . xv
Foreword by Anaar Niino . . . xxi

Introduction 1
    Our Journey Ahead   3
    The Modern Tradition of Witchcraft   4
    What Is a Sigil?   6
    What Is Sigil Magick?   6

Chapter 1: **A History of Mark Making** 9
    Eye—Brain—Hand—Art   9
    Signs, Symbols, and Societies   17
    Simple Yet Sophisticated, Sacred, and Secular   18
    A Picture Is Worth a Thousand Words ... or at Least One   22
    Embodying Symbols   27
    Gateway of the Divine   31
    The Timelessness of Tagging   34
    Symbol Genesis   36

Chapter 2: **The Meaning of the Mark** 37
    The Symbolism That Lives in Lines   38
    Basic Shapes and Signs   39
    Elements   75
    Directions   76
    Numbers   77

Zodiac and Astrological Signs   79

Letters   81

Colors   82

Other Symbol Systems   83

Finding Symbolism in Words: Building a Symbol Library   84

Chapter 3: **Making Magick** **91**

Understanding Magick and Spellcraft   91

How Does Drawing Sigils Work?   93

Uses for Sigil Witchery   95

Step by Step: How to Plan and Create Your Sigil   96

Applying Sigils, or Put a Sigil on It!   102

The Ritual Arts, or I Got That Witch a Ritual, Witches Love Ritual   103

The Vanishing Sigil   109

Sigils on Skin   118

Acknowledging Your Sigil   122

Devotional Sigils   123

Devotional Design Ritual   124

Sigils in Motion   125

Be Present in Your Body Exercise   127

Comparing Sigil Methods   129

Left Brain versus Right Brain?   131

Chapter 4: **Design Guidance** **135**

Setting Up for Sigil Witchery   135

An Instant Sacred Sphere   136

Getting Over Getting It Wrong   137

Simple versus Complex   138

Avoid Pictures and Pantomime   138

Why Draw Your Own Sigil?   139

Drawing Tech   140

About Tracing   141

Drawing Instructional   141

OMG Art Supplies!   148

Chapter 5: **Practice Exercises** 157

Scenarios   157

Solutions   162

Chapter 6: **Gallery** 179

The Power Sigil   179

Festival Sigils   183

The Artist's Sketchbook   187

Mago Djinn Sigil   190

Custom Sigils   191

The Mother Matrix   199

Other Artwork   202

Conclusion . . . 207

Resources . . . 209

Bibliography and Suggestions for Further Research . . . 211

Index of Symbols . . . 217

Illustrations and Photographs

Chapter 1

Montage of Images from Cave Paintings   11

Entoptic Phenomena   15

Cave Art Handprints and the Familiar Turkey Hand   16

Collection of Aboriginal Signs and Symbols   20

Evolution of the Chinese Character for *Cart* or *Wagon*   23

Egyptian Cartouche   24

An Array of Amazigh Symbols   29

Amazigh Tattoos   30

A Variety of Veves   33

Photo of Graffiti in Greece   35

Chapter 2

Point (Closed Dot)   39

Open Dot   40

Circle   40

Horizontal Line   41

Vertical Line   41

Dotted or Dashed Line   42

Diagonal Line   43

Cross   44

Chevron   45

X   46

Arrow   47

Wavy Line   48

Zigzag Line   49

Triangle   50

Square   51

Rectangle   52

Diamond   53

Crescent   54

Spiral   55

Pentagon   56

Hexagon   57

Other Polygons   58

Star   59

   Pentagram   59

   Hexagram   60

   Septagram   60

   Asterisk   61

Heart   62

Vesica Piscis or Mandorla   63

Eye   64

Infinity and Hourglass   65

Wheels and Shields   66

Wings   67

Key and Keyhole   68

Scales   69

Anchor   70

Butterfly   71

Hand   72

Spoon   73

Elements   74

Directions   76

Zodiac and Astrological Signs   79

Chapter 3

Photo of the Artist at Work   94

Donna's Sigil   100

Illuminating a Sigil with Traditional Pen and Ink on a Card   104

Vitality and *Vision* Spell Paintings by the Author   105

Sigil Satchels—Canvas Bags Embellished with Washable Paint by the Author   106

My "Power Sigil" Design, Embroidered and Photographed by Kohenet Ketzirah haMa'agelet   107

Wood, Bone, and Clay Make Great Bases for Sigil Pendants   108

A Chalk Sigil on a Doorstep   109

Earth Sigil   110

Water Sigil   111

A Sigil of Smoke   113

Planting a Sigil   115

For the Birds   116

Photo of the Author's Leg Tattoos   119

Sigils in Motion   126

Chapter 4

A Sacred Sphere of Energy   137

Drawing Circles and Ovals   142

Drawing Pentagrams   143

Drawing Six-Pointed Stars   144

Drawing Seven-Pointed Stars   145

Drawing Crescents   146

Drawing Spirals   147

Traditional Pen and Ink   152

Kinds of Brush Tips   154

Chapter 5

A Festival Sigil   163

A Coven Sigil   165

A Business Plan Sigil   167

An Office Ward Sigil   168

A Healing Sigil   169

A Transformational Sigil   170

A Sigil against Bullying   171

An Anti-Anxiety Sigil   172

A Fertility Sigil   173

A Focus Sigil   174

A Banishing and Binding Sigil   175

An Inspiration and Creativity Sigil   176

A Prosperity Sigil   177

Chapter 6

Upright Power Sigil   180

Inverted Power Sigil   181

PantheaCon Sigil   183

Paganicon Sigil   184

DragonCon Sigil   185

Workshop Sigil at Herne's Hollow in Delaware   186

Sigil Crafting and Notetaking   188

Another Sketchbook Page   189

Mago Djinn Sigil   190

Jaime's Sigil   191

Carolyn's Sigil   192

Jennifer's Sigil   193

Kim's Sigil   194

M's Sigil   195

Mary's Sigil   196

Matthew's Sigil   196

Megan's Sigil   197

Paul's Sigil   197

Stephanie's Sigil   198

Veronica's Sigil   198

The Drawing of the Mother Matrix   200

The Painting of the Mother Matrix   201

Details from Paintings from the Iconomage Series: *The Star Goddess* • *The Huntress* • *Hekate* •
   When Love Lay with Death and Darkness, Light Was Born   203

Familiar Territory   204

Queen of the Sabbat   205

The Shaman   206

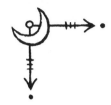

FOREWORD

BY ANAAR NIINO

What if, from the depths of your liminal consciousness, you could create your own symbolic language? What if you could create, from the ether, a personal language? What if you could create a magical language, a secret language?

What would you do with such a thing? Would you slip it under your pillow? Would you place it beneath a crib? Would you draw it in the air with smoke? Would you write it in lipstick?

What do I mean by *symbolic language*? It's a set of signs used to communicate all manner of things. The very words you're reading now are a set of agreed-upon signs. You can understand these words because you know what the agreement is. It is symbolic because when I write *apple* you understand what is meant by that set of abstract symbols. I do not need to draw an apple for you.

That is one form of symbolic language. It has its uses but is by far and large taken for granted. With lightning-fast imagery flashing before us, these symbols begin to lose their symbolic nature. They become divorced from their magical nature, losing their symbolism to become mechanical.

Sigils, on the other hand, are deeply personal. A sigil is an invented, private language, created for specific meanings known only to the creator. Agreement is not necessary for the symbol to take hold. Sigils reopen the symbolic and magical nature of a written form.

Can you draw something just for fun? Absolutely! But that form of symbolic art is a design and has other uses. That form of symbolism inhabits another part of our consciousness, one that is more present and readily accessible. It is not without meaning, as art is always meaningful in a variety of ways. But it is generally not meant for magical spiritual applications.

Sigils are very powerful tools coming from the very depths of our consciousness, reflecting our deepest desires. Sigils have a job to do. Sigils draw from deep within our psyche and are cast out into the world to do their work. The modern method of sigil making is by far the most effective means of drawing out those deep desires.

This book covers all those bases. Laura Tempest Zakroff offers a practical, non-threatening approach to sigil work. From advice on developing your own symbolic language to ideas on how to apply that sigil, a novice should feel very comfortable drawing their first sigil. There is plenty of room for creative self-expression, yet this book offers a solid, no-nonsense method to its magical applications.

Written in a conversational style, *Sigil Witchery* draws the veil and sweeps the cobwebs from the arcane. It exposes the mystery of sigil work for what it is: simple. Of course you may have heard me say, and will hear it again, that simple is not necessarily easy. But at least it's accessible.

So go now. Grab pen and paper, lipstick and mirror, stick and sand. Go grab something to draw with and make some magic.

—Anaar Niino
Grandmaster of the Feri Tradition
Archivist for the Victor and Cora Anderson Archive at the New Alexandrian Library

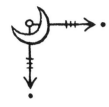 

INTRODUCTION

Imagine a large hotel meeting room packed to maximum capacity with all sorts of Pagans, displaying a wide range of ages, backgrounds, and experience. They'd chosen to attend this workshop on sigil magick over at least a dozen other options all happening at the same time on the busy convention schedule. Even though I've been teaching workshops on metaphysics, art, and dance for twenty years, I was battling a fair amount of anxiety. This was the very first time I'd be introducing my take on sigils to such a large audience. I was afraid that maybe they might not have read the description, and were expecting something more traditional. I flashed an image of a ceremonial magic seal on the overhead projector and gave this warning: "Okay, before we get started, if this is the kind of sigil you're expecting out of this workshop, now's the time to leave so you can catch another event. No hard feelings. I just don't want you to be disappointed. We're going to be looking at crafting sigils from a *very* different perspective." I waited. Not a single person budged. I took a deep breath and dove in. For the next ninety minutes, no one left the room. Afterward and all weekend long, people kept coming up to me asking when I would write a book on what I had presented.

That workshop kicked off a process that would be two years in the making—from the presentation at PantheaCon to this book first arriving on the shelves of bookstores everywhere. It's truly an amazing thing seeing what focused intent can accomplish!

I believe that every Witch has a certain talent that they excel at. Often we are good at many things, such as divination, spellcraft, mediumship, and counseling. But there's usually one specific area among those many hats we wear that is our niche, a skill where our ability to influence and change the world around us is paramount. Some Witches are incredible herbalists, their gardens lush and thriving. Others excel at kitchen witchery, mixing in their magick with meals. Or perhaps they have the gift of music, where their song enchants everyone around them.

For me, that talent involves the visual arts. I've been drawing and painting for as long as I can remember, and my parents fostered those abilities by enrolling me in art classes at the age of three. I continued to study fine art formally all the way through college. Whether it seemed a safer road to keep me occupied as a child (I got kicked out of gymnastics for not being coordinated enough) or my parents had some sort of a psychic insight, it was definitely the right road for me.

Early on, I perceived art as *my* way to understand and interact with the rest of the world. I have a distinct memory of me at age five scribbling rune-like shapes with my crayons on sheets of paper, one for each tree in our backyard. In my head, I believed the markings were for the protection of the trees. As I grew older, I reveled in drawing dragons and mermaids, telling myself elaborate stories about them as I painstakingly drew every little scale. From around age eight through eleven, I was an avid Egyptophile, not only learning about all of the mythology but also teaching myself to read and write hieroglyphics. Then I went further back to explore prehistoric cultures and early civilizations around the world—the remnants of their sculpture, architecture, paintings, and murals. As I studied more recent art history, I naturally gravitated toward the movements and artists whose work explored mythology and spirituality and reveled in symbolism: Gustave Moreau, Alphonse Mucha, Gustav Klimt, Marc Chagall, Frida Kahlo, Audrey Flack, and Andrew Wyeth, to name just a few.

The question was, how to create myth and magick in my own art? In college, I began to understand how I could use my art to explore myth, folklore, and religion. I explored the feminine and masculine divine through large hand-pulled prints and paintings. I experimented with deliberately casting spells through the making of art. I did independent studies on shrine making, divination, and trance techniques. I started to truly see the connection between the marks I made and the channeling of intent to get specific results. In the last two decades I've used my work to explore the space where magick and art intersect, and see how it actively influences my path as a Witch. I began to incorporate my own take on sigil magick into my drawings and paintings, following my instincts and drawing on years of art history studies.

People started to ask about my sigils, so I decided to reverse-engineer how I created them. (It may sound a bit odd that I needed to figure that out, but often when I'm making art, I'm following an internalized, subconscious formula.) Then I considered how others could use the same method to make their own sigils. It was this exploration that launched the workshops and this book.

OUR JOURNEY AHEAD

I came to sigil crafting from a very different direction and practice than the method that is most well known among magical practitioners. In fact, it wasn't until I was commissioned to do an illustration for a sigil magick article in *Witches & Pagans* magazine that I learned about the method popularized by chaos magicians.

The chaos magic method of creating a sigil involves composing a clarified statement. Next you remove all of the vowels and duplicate consonants, then scramble up the remaining letters to create the sigil. To finish the working, the sigil is typically burned after its creation. Or at least that's how the author of the article described their method and how it worked for them. (Some methods don't involve removing the vowels, but only the duplicate letters.)

I enjoyed illustrating the article, especially since it was well written and entertaining. It's a cool method, especially if it works for you. But that's not how I make sigils—as you're about to discover.

Instead, you're going to learn a process that I believe is more intuitive and fluid for right-brain thinkers and is very much grounded in Modern Traditional Witchcraft. How so? It is a fairly new and unique method for creating sigils, yet it pulls from basic skills our ancestors used to communicate prior to the advent of complex language. It can also be applied to a variety of metaphysical techniques, spellcraft approaches, and spiritual paths. Regardless of how artistic you may or may not consider yourself to be, this kind of sigil witchery is accessible to people with a wide variety of abilities and experiences.

To begin this journey, we will explore the work our ancestors have left us and try to decipher their mysteries, as well as illuminate the modern-day connections we can find in the symbols around us. I will introduce you to an extensive collection of marks, shapes, and symbols that will be the root of our sigils, and guide you in collecting others that hold meaning and power for you. Then we will explore how magick works, and see step by step how we can craft sigils for any situation. We will cover an extensive variety of ways we can implement and apply sigils for daily and ritual use. I'll go over design, practice, problem solving, supplies, and other technical aspects that will aid you in crafting your own sigils. I've also included practice scenarios where you can hone your skills and compare your work to some possible solutions. Lastly, I've included some of my own artwork and sigil witchery to inspire you, and provided some resources for you to continue your own research.

Before we launch into sigil space, first let's consider the framework for this method and go over some of the important basics of Witchcraft and sigils. Understanding the foundation and background for both is essential for starting off in the right direction.

THE MODERN TRADITION OF WITCHCRAFT

This title may seem like an oxymoron—how can something be modern *and* traditional? But I find it to be the perfect description for my path. I am a Modern Traditional Witch, blending the folklore, myths, and practices of my complex and diverse heritage with the acknowledgment that I am a modern person living in the United States.

Witchcraft—as a means to connect, see, and interact with the world—is as old as human civilization. I'm not talking about a specific organized religion, mystery school, family tradition, or degree system. Rather, I'm talking about the way of the Witch—the one who walks between worlds, talks with the spirits and deities, and manipulates the edges of consciousness. The word Witch, its connotation, and the identity of the practitioner may change from culture to culture, generation to generation, but the heart of magick is consistent throughout. (Nevertheless, the Witch persists.)

Over time we learn, collect, and build our practices, ideas, and traditions. As humanity progresses and makes new discoveries, we amend, shift, and grow as needed. We keep what works, we make note of what doesn't work, and we try new things. We can choose to make fire with flint and tinder, strike a match, or flick a lighter. We can use the power of the digital pixel to capture symbols thousands of years old, or draw new images with charcoal and our fingers. Intuition and instinct shake hands with ingenuity and imagination. This is the essence of the Modern Tradition of Witchcraft.

To guide the Witch's path, there are three keys:

Know Thyself: Be aware of your strengths and weaknesses, mentally, spiritually, and physically.

Maintain Balance: Balance is an idea, not a place. To understand it, we must consider the extreme points as well as moderation, and realize that all actions have a multitude of possible reactions.

Accept Responsibility: Be able to acknowledge, accept, and work with both the known and the unknown consequences of your actions and words.

It would be wise to keep these three concepts in mind when considering the focus, structure, and intended outcome of your sigil work. You need to be realistic about yourself and your environment, as well as mindful of both your limits and your possibilities for growth. You should think creatively about solutions and brainstorm possible outcomes and effects. And lastly, you should be willing to be responsible for your work in very real terms.

With this perspective in mind as our framework, let's explore the essentials of sigils.

What Is a Sigil?

First things first: How do you pronounce *sigil*? That may seem like a really basic question, but I find that it's a common one for many folks, especially if you're an avid reader and you rarely get to hear certain words pronounced out loud. It's also a logical place to start our study.

How dictionaries list the pronunciation: sijəl or 'si-jil

A more detailed explanation from an American perspective: The first *i* is soft, so it's like the *i* in Sidney, not long like in silence. The *g* is pronounced like a *j*, like in gem. The second *i* is an "eh" sound, as in gel. If you want to overthink it, there's somewhat of a phantom *d* hooked into the beginning of the *j* sound. If you don't want to overthink it, *sigil* rhymes with *vigil* (not to be confused with Virgil—the poet or the monkey).

Etymology: The word *sigil* derives from the Middle English *sigulle*, which comes from the Latin *sigillum*, meaning "seal." Another consideration is that it may be related to the Hebrew סגולה (*segula*), meaning a talisman, or a word or action of a spiritual nature.

I hope that helps you avoid seagulls and siggles. If you're still unsure, google *sigil* and the first result should be a brief definition with a sound icon. Click on the icon and you'll hear the correct pronunciation.

What Is Sigil Magick?

A sigil is a carved, drawn, or painted symbol that is believed to have magical properties. Magick is the art of focusing one's will or intent in order to bring about change. So sigil magick is creating specific symbols to influence a person, situation, or environment.

Many modern occultists and ceremonial magicians might have you believe that sigil magick belongs to the realm of "high magick"—that it is something intimidating, requiring arcane knowledge and maybe involving a membership to a secret society or three. Of course, when you're looking at certain sigils as a means to summon and control angels, demons, and other spirits, then it does often require having a background of understanding in those systems. So while that may be true of the form some magicians use, the art of sigil witchery is much more organic and has very humble, basic origins. In fact, you can find its roots in the earliest preserved magick known to humanity.

At the heart of sigil magick is the hand-drawn mark: lines, dots, and colors that form a symbol to designate space, conjure events, provide instructions, or invoke spirits and deities. From the outline of a hand-print drawn in red and yellow ochre on a cave wall, to temporary drawings made in the earth for sacred rites, to intricate carvings made on tools and jewelry, to murals on buildings, we have used our hands to make our mark on the world—seeking to influence it.

The Modern Tradition of Witchcraft has a very hands-on, no-nonsense approach to magick: do what needs to be done, when it needs to be done—without a lot of fancy trappings. (Everything else is just gravy on top.) This often means using whatever is on hand to do the work, instead of carefully curating ingredients and designing an elaborate ritual to coincide with the perfect alignment of the moon or stars. This immediacy is the essence of witchery to me. Sometimes just a bit of dirt, some string, and a match—or a ballpoint pen and a scrap of notebook paper—will do the trick when one's will is focused and the need is great.

Some folks may disdainfully call this approach "low magick." However, if you compare magick to computer technology, it's the low-level coding that is the closest to the source. The higher you get, the more you are moving away from the source, altering the language to suit other purposes. One method is not better than the other; they both get the work done in their own way. Both approaches certainly *do* work, so the trick is figuring out which one *you* are better suited for.

From simple to complex, from novice to artisan, there is plenty of room for learning how to create sigils of your very own. All it takes is a willingness to open up your imagination and the ability to make a mark. Remember back in school when you wondered just when geometry was going to come in handy in real life? Now's the time—and you're not being graded!

So set aside your fears, gather up some paper and a pen, and let's have some fun. It will be my pleasure to introduce you to the world of sigil witchery and help you learn to integrate it into your own practice.

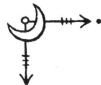

CHAPTER 1
A HISTORY OF MARK MAKING

I remember in nursery school working my little fingers through a shallow tray full of squishy poster paint, mixing the colors together—blending yellow and blue to make green, red and yellow to make orange—swirling it all about. Then I took my paint-covered hands and pressed them onto the clean paper provided, leaving behind two small imprints. The teacher hung up all of the papers on clothesline to dry, and we gazed up in awe at the colorful marks we had made, each set unique.

EYE—BRAIN—HAND—ART

As children, we revel in making art. We instantly recognize our ability to create new worlds, tell stories, recreate the world around us as we see it, and, most importantly, make our mark on the world. As we get older, we often push aside art making for other ways to get recognition from others, to explain ourselves and our world. We may forget that we even knew how to draw or paint or to play make-believe. Yet it was these very "simple" skills that we humans first embraced to begin our journey toward civilization. No matter how sophisticated we may perceive ourselves to be now, our ability to visualize ideas and draw symbols is what first set us apart on the evolution timeline. In her book *The First Signs*, Genevieve Von Petzinger writes: "The first instance of making an intentional graphic mark was one of the profoundly important moments in our species' history—right up there with the invention of tools, the control of fire, and the development of spoken language."[1]

It can be easy for some to dismiss drawing and painting as something frivolous. But if you really think about it, the process and the background behind it is incredible. We observe the world around us and translate 3-D into 2-D through a series of marks, colors, and shapes. Or we picture something in our brain—literally something that has no physical form outside of our head—and draw it into reality. Manifestation comes from seeing with our eyes and picturing in our brain, then creating through and with our hands. The evolutionary leap that our brains needed to develop in order to see, think, and create intentional marks is a phenomenal thing. Our ability to think abstractly, envision time and space, and translate our world into new forms is what helped set us apart as a whole new species thousands upon thousands of years ago.

Most people are familiar with the amazing cave paintings in Spain and France depicting herds of bison and horses. But few people, including archaeologists and anthropologists, have turned their gaze to the other human-made marks found in those very same caves. Those overlooked marks and symbols caught the attention of researcher Genevieve Von Petzinger, who has spent the last several years exploring caves all throughout Europe. She documented every single mark she could find and put them into a database. In TED talks and in her book *The First Signs*, she explains how she found thirty-two signs that appear again and again in caves thousands of miles apart. Not only that, but their making also spanned centuries, suggesting meaningful use over time. Her research points to the likelihood that a symbolic tradition developed in Africa long before our ancestors journeyed forth into other parts of the world. This theory could certainly explain the similarities we see in the early art of Europe, Indonesia, and Australia.

Why would our ancestors create a system of symbols and migrate with them? I think the reason is pretty easy to determine: the desire to communicate and to connect. Considering the amount of effort required to carve an object or paint in a dark crevice of a cave, it's clear that they were pur-

---

1. Genevieve Von Petzinger, *The First Signs* (New York: Atria Books, 2016), 174.

posefully making marks with the intent to communicate meaning (even if the precise meaning may be lost to us now).

Montage of Images from Cave Paintings

When we look at the historical timeline of communication technology, we can see the direct correlation with the evolution of society. Some of the earliest tools found in caves were used to crush and mix pigments into paint and apply them to surfaces—meaning we could collect pigments from different places and take them with us. There's the making of papyrus and other forms of paper to replace heavy stone and clay tablets, making it easy to transport images and words. Advancements in bookbinding all the way through to the printing press all come back to that desire to spread ideas, share information, and collect knowledge. Starting in the late nineteenth century, telephones and telegraphs helped us connect over long distances more immediately. The twentieth century saw the development of computers, television, and the internet, leading to the information revolution we have today, where tiny hand-held devices allow us to share ourselves with the world through pictures, words, and video. Even today, we still rely on symbols and images to express ourselves and communicate with the world around us.

Many of our modern symbols share shape and form with those thirty-two signs Von Petzinger documents. Those signs include the asterisk (six-pointed star shape), cruciforms (cross and X shapes), half-circles, straight lines, dots, chevrons, crosshatches, triangles, finger fluting (lines left by fingers in soft surfaces such as clay and mud), zigzags, spirals, quadrangles (four-sided shapes), handprints, ovals, scalariforms (ladderlike shapes), penniforms (feather shapes), circles, cordiforms (heart shapes), and serpentiforms (snakelike, wavy lines). Von Petzinger explores a wide variety of possibilities for how and why these signs were used: to mark territory, to pass along messages, to tell stories, for ritual and magic, for worship and observance, etc. What is most important to Von Petzinger is not pinpointing the exact interpretations of these signs, but rather recognizing that they are "the product of a fully modern mind, one capable of great abstraction and symbolic thought."[2] What matters is not the meaning of the symbols, but the fact that we humans made them—simultaneously marking our place on the evolutionary ladder.

---

2. Genevieve Von Petzinger, *The First Signs* (New York: Atria Books, 2016), 268.

Even if we were able to figure out the exact meaning of one collection of symbols from a certain area, it is very likely that the meaning of the signs changed over time and location, varying from group to group. We don't even have to dig very far back in the historical record to find evidence of these fluctuations. For example, consider the crosshatch shape. I grew up with it being called the pound sign on the touch-tone phone and the number sign in math class. My husband—a musician—would be more inclined to see it as the sharp symbol, denoting a note played a half step higher. Now it's commonly called a hashtag and is used for tracking social media trends by keywords on the internet. Imagine if I showed a young child the rotary desk phone my grandparents had. They would probably have great difficulty trying to figure it out, wondering how someone could text and tag with that thing!

Without a codex or complete historical record, it's hard to know for sure what many of those early symbols meant to our ancestors, as well as how and why they used them as they did. It's possible that they carved and painted them on everything (themselves, their clothes, buildings), but we only have what's been left behind over time to go by thanks to the protective environment of caves. Many of the best examples of cave paintings do not occur in areas that also show evidence of regular human habitation. That information suggests that those caves may have been sacred places, which lends credence to the idea that the art may have had spiritual and magical connotations.

How so, you may ask? The stylized images of those enormous round bison and galloping horses could be aligned with what some anthropologists and art historians call "hunting magic." Hunting magic falls in the realm of sympathetic magick. This is the idea that like affects like, and that the microcosm can bring change in the macrocosm—influencing the whole through the association with or manipulation of the part. So by painting well-fed prey and depicting a successful hunt, our ancestors may have believed that their metaphysical work would bring their desire to fruition. We could interpret the signs surrounding the animals as weapons, animal and hunter tracks, and simulated woundings.

But that explains only a small percentage of cave paintings and carvings, as we can find many paintings of animals *without* those hunting marks and signs. We also find those same symbols in places without depictions of animals—so hunting magic may not be the actual reason they were made.

Another possible explanation can be found in David Lewis-Williams's work on exploring shamanism and cave art. His research suggests that there are seven abstract shapes that are manifested through what is called *entoptic phenomena*. The word *entoptic* derives from the Greek words for "within" and "vision," so entoptic phenomena refers to visual effects whose source is within the eye itself and the brain—meaning not caused by outside visual stimuli. Those seven shapes are dots, half-circles, spirals, zigzags, parallel lines, wavy lines, and grids (or crosshatches)—all designs that are also found in cave art across the world. Maybe the cave artists were drawing shapes they were seeing in trance and dream visions. So perhaps that is another kind of esoteric activity, connecting the making of these shapes with trances and shamanic journeys.

Or maybe there's another explanation, one connected to identity. In my opinion, one of the most powerful symbols found in cave art is the handprint. The handprints were made in two ways: by pressing the hand against the wall and outlining it with pigment, and by painting the hand liberally with pigment and "printing" it onto the wall. Handprints are often seen in layers on top of each other, in a wide range of sizes—cluing us in that they were made by people of all ages and genders. So not just shamans or artists but everyone may have had a hand in making the symbols. I see handprints as one of the simplest ways to make your own unique mark on the world. It says to everyone, "I exist, I was here." Even today, this meaning is apparent as we teach our children to fingerpaint and to press their hands into clay so they can see the marks left behind. They are taught the transformable nature of their own bodies when we show them how to change the outline of their own hand into other shapes (such as turkeys!).

Entoptic Phenomena

Cave Art Handprints and the Familiar Turkey Hand

We can also see correlations in other, more modern artistic practices that may hint at what our ancestors were up to. The repetition of symbols and patterns found on walls, tools, jewelry, and figurines and in burial sites—when compared to similar designs found in modern systems—suggests ownership markings, landscape exploration/mapping, tribal identification, personal rank or station indication, talismans and protective powers, decorative purposes, mnemonic devices, and storytelling. So let's look at some more relatively recent examples of symbol systems we *do* know the meaning of, and use them to see the threads connecting us to our ancestors and each other.

Signs, Symbols, and Societies

Before we explore some wonderful examples from several symbol systems, let's take a moment to think about some words. *Symbol*, *sign*, *sigil*, *seal*, *motif*, *design*, and *image* are usually all found as synonyms. (I'll be using them throughout the text so that in some places you're not reading the same word over and over again.) They all connect seeing something visually and assigning it meaning or importance, but there are some nuances worth noting:

- A **sign** represents or points to an idea in a fairly straightforward way. Think road signs, ads, etc.
- A **symbol** is similar to a sign, but it tends to represent something more profound, complex, or abstract than itself, and may have a hidden meaning or truth.
- A **sigil** is a carved, drawn, or painted symbol that is believed to have magical properties or power.
- A **seal** is a mammal that lives by the water. (Just seeing if you were still paying attention!) A seal is a mark that displays authenticity, demonstrates authority, or keeps something safe or secret.
- A **motif** is a recurring and distinctive form or shape that is repeated in a design or pattern.
- A **design** is a thoughtfully organized structure of elements in a work of art.
- An **image** is a physical likeness or otherwise visual representation of a person, place, thing, or idea.

I'm introducing these subtleties to you so you can consider them as you view the upcoming illustrations and think about how each culture uses their art.

I feel it's also very important to note that I'm not showing you the following examples from symbol systems to say "These are sigils" or "Make stuff like this culture." I'm including them in order to demonstrate the similarities in line, mark, shape, and usage between diverse cultures and time frames. You can appreciate the work without appropriating it, and recognize its commonality. If you are interested in any system (either the ones introduced here or others), I thoroughly encourage you to do more research on the cultures surrounding them. Also, if you have roots in a system shown here, I hope you find new inspiration and perspective—maybe a new angle or area to study on your path.

SIMPLE YET SOPHISTICATED, SACRED, AND SECULAR

Whether considering symbols in cave paintings, medieval manuscripts, or modern art, it's vital that we understand that essentially the same brain made them all. Despite the advances in science and technology and the exploration of thought over the passage of time, we are not physically or mentally more advanced in the present day. We are just as prone to superstition today as we are capable of logic. Thinking of our ancestors as less advanced or intelligent is just as farfetched a notion as romanticizing people today who look or live different from ourselves. We may have different experiences and appearances, but we're all human—and we often turn to symbols for the very same reasons.

So even if we can't determine exactly why cave paintings were made, I think it's safe to say that the symbols held deep meaning to the people who made them. And those people weren't that different from us. Why? Because when we find similar symbols elsewhere in the world, still used by living societies, they're inherently complex and highly sophisticated despite their apparent simplicity.

To understand this relationship, we will first look to the art of the Aboriginals—the indigenous people of Australia. According to numerous archaeological discoveries, for *at least* the last 50,000 years a multitude of diverse tribes have flourished on the continent and surrounding areas. Much of their art and its meanings have managed to survive, despite the effects of the last two hundred years of white colonization. The concept of having certain people specialize in making art is a newer idea to the Aboriginals—art had always been such an intricate part of daily life that all people were involved in the process of making it: baskets, weavings, carvings, body painting, sand drawings, tool making, dancing, etc. These traditions continue to evolve today through modern Aboriginal artists in both traditional and new media.

Many of the symbols found in Aboriginal art clearly have a basis as signs relaying important survival information. There are the marks fashioned after animal tracks: a chevron with a center line to represent emu footprints, opposing J shapes for kangaroo prints, and a fringed serpentine line to represent the impression left by the goanna (a large lizard). Other symbols represent the bodies of the animals themselves: groupings of small dots for ants, larger ovals for eggs, thick wavy lines for snakes, and connected rings to represent grubs. Then there are the signs that mark landscape features that are important to survival. Concentric circles and spirals are used to mark the locations of watering holes, and they're connected by parallel wavy lines if there's running water between them. Meeting places are also marked with concentric circles, but are surrounded by diagonal lines that point toward the center. There are also the symbols for hunting equipment, based on simplified outlines of spears, shields, and boomerangs. Other symbols are much more stylized, such as an inverted U to symbolize a person, which is then paired with various configurations of vertical lines to represent a man or a woman, as well as their age.

For the majority of symbols found in Aboriginal art, their similarities to recognizable tracks, features, and animals—as well as the fact that we're dealing with a *living* culture with a long history that still uses these symbols—might lead us to believe that the meanings are pretty straightforward and consistent. Culture is constantly evolving, and Australia is a huge place, with different landscapes and challenges in each area. Some symbols gain new meaning as hunters and gatherers become farmers, doctors, and lawyers—and others lose meaning. It's also important to recognize that these shapes become the inspiration for patterns of decoration and elements of magick and rituals. Dots may build from the shape of a tiny ant and can signify the presence of ants, but ants can also represent colonies, movement, and small things have a larger impact over time. Concentric circles and spirals can mark the physical location of a watering hole, but they also symbolize the life-giving power of water, the ebb and flow of life, and a place where everyone gathers. The multiplicity of meaning illustrates the importance of not taking everything so literally. We must also remember that although symbols can look similar, they may have different meanings to other people.

Collection of Aboriginal Signs and Symbols

It's also important not to fall into the trap of perceiving Aboriginal art (or any of the art we will talk about) as "primitive." There is nothing primitive or simplistic about abstracting the world around us. Eurocentric anthropologists, archeologists, and historians have done a spectacularly horrid job over the last several centuries of diminishing the work of cultures not found on their continent. While making accurately representational art may seem like it requires a lot of skill, it takes a deeper sense of creativity to see the world in non-representational terms. This deeper vision includes everything from using shapes, colors, and patterns to express spiritual and dreamlike experiences to elongating and exaggerating bodies to express movement and divine presence. Making an accurate representation of something takes careful observation, while creating abstraction requires a significant use of imagination.

A great example of abstract use of Aboriginal symbols outside of depicting daily activities and living is when they are used to describe what is known in English as "the Dreaming." The Dreaming is an idea that encompasses a way to describe all that is known and liminal, the origin and subsequent mythology of the people. It explains life, living, being, and dying, and how everything is interconnected. In his book *Images of Power*, David Lewis-Williams remarks that art making is integral to Aboriginal religious experience and aesthetics. He writes that the "great theme of Bushman art is the power of animals to sustain and transform human life by affording access to otherwise unattainable spiritual dimensions."[3]

It's interesting to note that in some instances of exploring the idea of the Dreaming, symbols are meant to be lasting marks, and in other uses they are meant to be temporary. There are signs engraved in stone or painted on canvas to tell important stories, physically signify or mark sacred sites, and describe mythic forces. But those same symbols—such as spirals and wavy lines—can be found painted on bodies, for both decoration and ritual use. There are also large-scale ground paintings created especially for ritual use by the practitioners. Again, commonly utilized basic symbols and images may be used, but it is believed that they become supernaturally enhanced during the ceremony and should

3. David Lewis-Williams and Thomas Dowson, *Images of Power: Understanding Bushman Rock Art* (Johannesburg: Southern Book Publishers, 1989), Preface.

be destroyed afterward. But that only happens with those certain ritual processes. The same symbol drawn for another purpose isn't changed metaphysically and doesn't need to be destroyed.[4]

This duality means that although a symbol might be used in the context of sacred ritual, Aboriginal artists use the same symbols in the mundane world as well. They're not tied exclusively to sacred application because there isn't such a hard line between the spiritual and the secular. Lewis-Williams explains: "For the Bushman, religion is not a separate part of life to be indulged in only on certain solemn and ritual occasions. It is part of the fabric of everyday existence: no clear line is drawn between sacred and secular. This is one of the reasons why their beliefs about and attitude toward the supernatural are important for a proper understanding of their art."[5]

I think one of the most valuable lessons to take away from Aboriginal art is the accepted fluidity between mundane and spiritual images. A single symbol can exist in both worlds; its meaning and application is inherent to the person making or using it. It is their belief that guides the meaning for that moment or application—and that can be as obvious and concrete or as spirit-driven and mysterious as the maker intends it to be. This relationship between the symbol and the artist is one you'll want to keep in mind when it's time to get down to some sigil witchery.

A Picture Is Worth a Thousand Words ... or at Least One

One of the primary benefits of symbols and signs is that they simplify complex ideas. A single picture can represent a whole situation and be quickly understood for those who are in the know. Those early symbols on cave walls most likely were not meant to be letters of an alphabet or random scribbles, but rather were probably part of pictographic or ideographic systems. The symbols become signs and messages not just for the people who make them but also for others to see later and respond to.

---

4. For a good online resource on Aboriginal art by Aboriginals, I recommend checking out http://aboriginalart.com.au.

5. David Lewis-Williams and Thomas Dowson, *Images of Power: Understanding Bushman Rock Art* (Johannesburg: Southern Book Publishers, 1989), 13.

We can look to language to get a glimpse into the connection between symbols, words, meanings, and usage. Over time, pictograms may have evolved into logographic writing systems, where glyphs represent words and sounds rather than the things they resemble. For example, with Egyptian hieroglyphs, you have a line of glyphs that clearly look like an animal or item, but they don't read as "ibis, man, duck, eye, scarab, staff, staff." How each glyph is placed—what it is located next to or what it is above or below—alters the meaning.

This makes context all the more important to consider. You can't just pull a single symbol out of a group to grasp its complete meaning; you need to see the whole picture and the interrelations. It's also fascinating to note that both ancient Egyptian hieroglyphs and early Chinese scripts have this structure in common. Especially with Chinese characters, we can observe their long preserved history as they evolved from originally looking like the things they stand for. They became increasingly stylized and streamlined as time progressed, which essentially cut down on the amount of time required to make each character. In the illustration shown here of the evolution of the Chinese character for *cart* or *wagon*, note the resemblance to an actual cart on the left, and how it becomes more stylized as it evolves to the right.

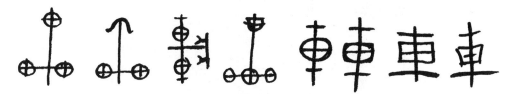

Evolution of the Chinese Character for *Cart* or *Wagon*

Very rarely does a single glyph from a logographic script represent a complete idea like a crafted symbol or pictogram does. It's more like a letter, a sound, part of something much larger. Keep this in mind when crafting sigils. A dot, line, or star gains more complex meaning as it relates to the other shapes and marks placed around it.

One way to see this in action is in Egyptian cartouches, which started to appear early in the Fourth Dynasty during the rule of Pharaoh Sneferu. A cartouche is a group of hieroglyphics encased in an elongated shen ring (an oval-like shape with a single flattened end), and originally signified a royal name. Cartouches are found on amulets and are carved as protective seals on tombs. The closed shape of the oval surrounding the hieroglyphics acts as a border of sympathetic magick—it protects the name, therefore it protects the bearer of that name. Nowadays you can get your own name made into a cartouche (even if you're not considered royalty) to bring you protection and good luck.

Egyptian Cartouche

If we consider the word *hieroglyphic*, we also get a hint of divine inspiration. It originates from the Greek *hieros* ("sacred") + *glyphe* ("carving"). Therefore hieroglyphics could be viewed as sacred writing/images. An instance where we might see a connection between hieroglyphics and the sacred power of words is with the Hebrew alphabet. It is considered to be one of the most ancient alphabets and has long been associated with having a sacred context in Jewish culture. The actual history between the Jews and Egypt is a hot topic of debate both in biblical and archaeological circles, but the similarities between the symbols and letters are quite apparent.[6]

What's most relevant here though is the use of the Hebrew alphabet for magic—in both an ancient and a modern context. There are many examples of supernatural workings in the Torah (the holy texts of Judaism), but most people are familiar with the stories of King Solomon from the Book of Kings. There are numerous tales of his magical exploits, but the one most relevant here was about his God-given ring that bore a special seal, giving him the power to control *djinn* (or *spirits* or *demons*, depending on the translation). King Solomon's story also provides inspiration for Jewish mysticism and other magical texts much further down the line that seek power through symbols such as those found in the Kabbalah and the *Key of Solomon*. The term *Kabbalah* refers to a branch of Jewish mysticism believed to have emerged in France and southern Spain in the twelfth or thirteenth century. It focuses on "the inner structure and processes taking place within the divine realms, on whose metaphysical dynamics the Kabbalists tried to exert influence."[7] Kabbalistic principles suggest that since the Hebrew language has divine origins, one can take a specific name, note the characters that make up that name, and use mathematical correlations and geometry as a formula to implement magic with that name. It is likely that the work of the Kabbalists influenced the writer/s of the *Key of Solomon*, a grimoire that surfaced around the fourteenth or fifteenth century during the Italian Renaissance. The *Key of Solomon*

---

6. See the fascinating comparison chart at "History of the Hebrew Alphabet," https://en.wikipedia.org/wiki/History_of _the_Hebrew_alphabet.

7. Dr. Agata Paluch, "The Power of Language in Jewish Kabbalah and Magic: How to Do (and Undo) Things with Words," Feb. 29, 2016, www.bl.uk/hebrew-manuscripts/articles/the-power-of-language-in-jewish-kabbalah#sthash.NrP5zEMk.dpuf.

serves as an instructional manual on the magical arts—and there is also the *Lesser Key of Solomon*, compiled around the seventeenth century with a similar intent. Kabbalistic theories and sacred geometry as well as both *Keys* can be seen as greatly influencing many traditions of ceremonial magic for the last five hundred years. It's through those various orders that a number of sigil practices developed, so closely linked with Hebrew magical theories that in many a modern ceremonial magic grimoire you'll still find sigils with Hebrew characters incorporated into them.

But let us not fall down into the ceremonial magic rabbit hole! (There are links in the "Bibliography and Suggestions for Further Research" section if you'd like to study any of these historical documents online.) Let's circle back to the power of the word, symbol, image—and religion.

So in Egypt we have the development of picture-words alongside a rich history of sculpture, murals, and other pictorial arts. Representational images were commonly made both to honor the gods and to record daily life, and the Egyptians have an extensive timeline of pictorial art making. Despite its early connection to hieroglyphics, the Hebrew alphabet distinctly moved away from recognizable images. This stylistic development is likely linked to the second of the Ten Commandments, which prohibits the making of "graven" images and the worshiping of idols. A similar ban is found in Islam against portraying the human form, as it borders on idolatry. Instead, both Jews and Muslims put their mystical artistic energy into the written word, and the power of symbols. In Judaism, there is a rich history of ritual objects (chalices, scroll casings, reading implements) being heavily engraved or carved with symbolic designs based on Hebrew letters to make them pleasing to God—setting them aside as sacred objects. In Islam, we see words combined with sacred geometry to create elaborate designs and motifs that evoke the divine in everything from architecture and vessels to rugs and jewelry. If we look at the Arabic alphabet, it too (like Hebrew) is not designed to remind us of images, yet it is incredibly graceful and beautiful to look at. Whole mosques are covered with sacred words and combined with geometric designs to form patterns, instead of using representational images. Even when religion tries to forbid it, humanity still finds ways to use art to expand consciousness and connect with divinity and the world around us.

Embodying Symbols

If we move westward from Egypt and the nearby Arabian Peninsula, we will find the Amazigh people, more commonly known as the Berbers, who are indigenous to North Africa. They live throughout the entirety of the region and are believed to have resided there since at least 10,000 BCE. There are numerous cave paintings and rock art in the mountains of Algeria and in the Sahara that were most likely created by the ancestors of today's Amazigh people. Although the majority of modern-day Amazigh are Sunni Muslim, the practices in some regions point to pre-Islamic religious beliefs rooted in polytheism as well as animism and ancestor veneration. Many of the tribes are or were nomadic, so they have been traders of culture and art for much of their existence. It is possible that through their amazing symbolic art, we can get another peek into history.

As with the Aboriginals, art is deeply intrinsic to Amazigh life, with symbols prevalent and powerful throughout the culture. In their book *Imazighen: The Vanishing Traditions of Berber Women*, Margaret Courtney-Clarke and Geraldine Brooks note, "The Berber languages have been fragmented by time and distance, but the language of symbols remains. Dialects differ, but the symbols that Berbers use in their jewelry, pottery, weavings, and even tattoo into their flesh are the same in the valleys of Algeria's Kabylia ranges, on the peaks of Morocco's High Atlas, and in the deserts of Tunisia."[8] Not just mere decoration, the symbols cover the walls in homes and are woven into tapestries, rugs, and clothing, painted onto pottery, and made into talismanic jewelry—all to protect the people who use them in every aspect of their daily lives.

Amazigh people—especially the women—have been applying tattoos to their bodies for thousands of years, long before the rise of Islam. Most commonly seen marking the chin, cheeks, and forehead of the face, tattoos may also be applied to the arms, legs, breasts, back, thighs, and pubic triangle. There is a modern misconception that the tattoos were applied to the faces of women to make them unattractive to invading soldiers in the nineteenth century, but the practice long

---

8. Margaret Courtney-Clarke (photographer), with essays by Geraldine Brooks, *Imazighen: The Vanishing Traditions of Berber Women* (New York: Clarkson Potter Publishers, 1996), 78.

predates that idea. *Al Jazeera* writer Yasmin Bendaas reports of the tradition: "The tattoos were considered enhancers of beauty when applied to the face and had therapeutic and healing purposes—particularly related to fertility—when found elsewhere on the body, such as above the ankle or on the back of the hand. For men, traditional tattoos were far less ornamental and served healing purposes."[9] The tattoos can denote tribe, lineage, and rank, as well as carry symbols of protection, strength, fertility, and luck. Bendaas also notes that "these symbols embody a more general preservation, not only of women, but also of the land. With tattoos containing literal depictions of nature such as partridges, gazelles and camels, ties to the environment are abundant." Unfortunately, as Islam prohibits the practice of tattooing, this way of women marking themselves has largely fallen out of practice, but it does still exist today.

What is especially interesting is that while there are some Amazigh symbols that definitely resemble what they're supposed to mean, a great many of them are incredibly abstract—to the point where if we were not able to talk to the actual people who make them, we'd be just as much at a loss about their meaning as we are about those early signs in the caves. They also seem very simplistic, with their combinations of dots, triangles, cross marks, and chevrons, yet once again we're looking at a very sophisticated and artful system. Just because a motif may have its roots in the daily aspects of life—hair combs, lamps, fish, snakes, grains, and insects, for example—doesn't limit its meaning just to that obvious relation. Birds can symbolize freedom and travel, seeds and plants often speak to fertility and prosperity, and tools such as anchors and sickles are often used for protection.

As the Amazigh people cover such a large region, some symbols definitely do vary in style and meaning from tribe to tribe. Another explanation for the differences, as well as the level of abstraction, most likely has to do with how much Islam has been integrated into that tribe. In groups that have been more isolated from modern Islam, the markings are often more recognizable as plants, animals, tools, and heavenly bodies. This kind of art speaks to the polytheistic and animistic roots

---

9. Yasmin Bendaas, "Algeria's Tattoos: Myths and Truths," *Al Jazeera*, August 11, 2013, www.aljazeera.com/indepth/features /2013/08/201386134439936719.html.

of the people. The people are not shy about connecting with the sacredness of the land and sky, the plants and animals. The symbols represent and call upon that connection through tattoos, adornment, and household goods. The motifs are believed to carry the blessings and energies of the things they represent.

An Array of Amazigh Symbols

Amazigh Tattoos

In contrast, in cities and areas where Islam is the law, the markings have evolved to become more abstract and seen more as design elements. There is still an undertone of connection, but it has been modified to work within the confines of the new religion. The meaning may still be there, even if the representational image is not. Again, we see the evolution of symbols at work in living cultures, shifting with the modern-day people who apply and evolve those symbols over time.

GATEWAY OF THE DIVINE

If we travel south out of Morocco and Algeria into Western Sahara, Mali, and Niger, we find ourselves along the trade routes of the Berbers known as the Tuareg. The Tuareg are best known for their blue-colored clothing and incredible metalworking skills, evidenced in their amulets and talismans. It's possible that out of their desire for more jewelry-making materials they extended their trading further into the heart of Central Africa, the Congo, and even as far east as Ethiopia.

The native people of these areas are well known for their own kind of distinctive symbolism and artistry, such as *nsibidi*, an ideographic script used by the Ekoi, Efik, and Igbo peoples for wall designs, shields, swords, tattoos, and more. Then we have the Kongo people, known for their incredible carved masks and *nkisi* (sacred) statues to venerate the ancestors, spirits, and guardians of places. When we look at some of the designs and markings found in the iconic Tuareg amulets, there is a sense that the artisans were (and are) likely inspired by the arts of these regions. The jewelry is a mix of Amazigh symbols and artistry with the aesthetic of nsibidi, the designs steeped in an awareness of communion with spirits.

However, while the Tuareg may have found inspiration to add to their own designs, we're going to leave behind the continent of Africa and head to the New World to look at symbols born out of the diaspora: the religious symbols known as *veves*. The combination of nsibidi and the arts and beliefs of the Kongo people seem to be the exported root of this tradition of powerful mark making born in the harshest conditions. Although the origins of veves are difficult to trace, looking at similarities between veves, nsibidi markings, and spiritual practices of the Kongo, it's likely they came to the Americas with people who were taken from those regions and sold into the slave trade.

Out of the crucible of forced Christianity, families broken and tribes ripped apart, and cruel living conditions, along with the infusion of indigenous practices, the religion of Vodou and the practice of veves emerged.

A veve is Vodou symbol dedicated to a *lwa* (spirit) that is drawn on the floor in a ritual context to bring the spirit physically into the space. It is *not* a sigil in the context of the way that certain sigils are used in ceremonial magic to command a demon, daemon, djinn, or similar spiritual entity. Rather, the veve is a gateway of manifestation for the lwa, an act of reverence, welcome, and devotion. There is no exact "only" veve design for any given lwa either, but there tends to be a base element or motif associated with that spirit accented with additional markings that vary from house to house.

Somewhat similar to the Aboriginal ground paintings used during ritual, the veve that is drawn on the ground is meant to be temporary—it's often drawn in powder (cornmeal, ash, and other ingredients). Veves may be constructed in other ways (artwork, hangings, flags, etc.) for non-ritual devotional practices. Another thing to consider about the fleeting nature of the drawn veve and its history: if you are forced into a situation where it's illegal or even punishable by death to practice your religion, but you refuse to submit, it is very advantageous to be able to depict divine entities in a drawing that can be quickly erased at a moment's notice. That's the power of symbol and belief. The temporary nature of veves in ritual is also a way to make sure the door to the other world is properly closed as well after everything is done. That way nobody is hanging out in the gateway past the time expected. The nature of the veve and its connection to being a gateway and devotional symbol is vital to understand. It's more than just a pretty design—it's a sacred act.

It's important to remember that Vodou is a living, breathing practice, just as the Aboriginals and Amazigh are still creating new art and symbols. Nothing is under a lens or trapped under a pin like a specimen. Veves are not to be copied for the sake of looking cool, but should be understood and respected in the context of symbols and evolving culture. What we can take away from the use of veves is that symbols can be used to communicate with divine forces and crafted in acts of devotion. We can also note the effect, meaning, and power behind creating a temporary mark and a permanent one, as well as use in private and public environments.

A Variety of Veves

THE TIMELESSNESS OF TAGGING

On the other side of the spectrum, let's consider signs and symbols that are generally made in secret yet are meant to buck authority in subtle *or* blatant ways—ones that are often meant to leave a permanent mark, often to the chagrin of others. This mark-making technique is known as *graffiti*.

Graffiti (singular: *graffito*) is an Italian word meaning "incised inscription or design," so it could refer to any kind of carved design or message. However, it has come to be equated more often with anonymous, unauthorized markings—carved, drawn, or painted—made on surfaces.

Graffiti is a kind of art that is made in defiance against what is expected or allowed. It is a worldwide phenomenon, the symbolic art of the disenfranchised and the marginalized, those of the counterculture. *Tagging* (repeating a design, name, or message in multiple places) is a way of marking territory and triggering identity, a way of saying to the world, "Hey, I exist here too, even if you refuse to see me." It's commonly seen as vandalism rather than art, since it tends to be done on the places and property of others, though it would be unfair to say graffiti artists revel in desecrating or destroying their neighbors' property. Most graffiti is found on things that could be considered liminal spaces: on back-alley walls, underpasses, rail cars, and abandoned buildings. It shows up in semi-communal spaces: parks, subway walls, and bathroom doors. Whether in words or images, the graffiti is a message from the maker to the world, aimed at communicating with it at large.

What's especially interesting about graffiti is that a design rarely is done just once. Often a certain symbol or message is repeated again and again, either from constantly being reapplied after its removal and/or from being duplicated in multiple locations. This kind of tagging can mark a specific range of territory for a group, designate a meeting place, or invite a response from others. Members of various secret societies, underground groups, and gangs have all used graffiti to connect with one another as well. Lining up the locations of repetitive markings can sometimes create a larger picture, a constellation, map, or message the artist wants to subtly make known. There's even a very modern design called the *Linking Sigil* (aka *LS* or *Ellis*) that was designed in the early

2000s for magical practitioners to mark places of power and link them together to stimulate change in the larger society.[10]

Photo of Graffiti in Greece

Guerrilla graffiti installations are frequently done by artists seeking to make loud social or political statements or to transform the face of buildings in blighted inner cities and war-torn landscapes. They ask the viewer to question their reality, authority, and social standards. The power is in the

---

10. For more about the Linking Sigil, see Assault on Reality, www.dkmu.org.

ability to make a work of graffiti appear overnight, and to accept that it may be destroyed soon after its making, though in many cities across the world, graffiti artists are now being hired to purposely bring their art to the masses in public spaces. Therein lies the question: Is graffiti made with permission still revolutionary? Does being sanctioned take away its power? Or does this new form of sanctioned graffiti become something else—another form of transformational art? It's certainly an interesting challenge for the graffiti artist to consider.

As graffiti is found all over the world and has been made for centuries, it's another connecting point for the human need to make signs and symbols. It also speaks to the power and thrill of making art that's unexpected and out-of-bounds, creating hidden messages in plain sight, and making repetitive symbols. Graffiti elicits the power of the subliminal, the subversive, and the bold. These are important things to keep in mind when we discuss crafting sigils: Who are we speaking to? What is our message?

SYMBOL GENESIS

There are many more symbol systems from around the world (ancient to modern) that I haven't mentioned here. To cover them all would require a whole book, not just a chapter. Rather, I hope that through the systems we *have* covered here, you are noticing the commonality of markings, the variety of uses, and the fluent nature of their meanings. Cultures thousands of miles and/or centuries apart can come to create similar-looking symbols with almost identical meanings—or very different ones. It's imperative to consider the cultural context and application to fully understand the nature and meaning of the marks and signs we see in the world. The challenge I present to you is to deeply consider what meanings you find in symbols, and how to make signs that are your own.

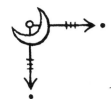

CHAPTER 2

THE MEANING OF THE MARK

Your name is a collection of letters making up the words that identify you: your first name, last name, maybe a middle name or two, or a nickname. It may be the name you were born with, a name you were given, a name you added or changed, or one you took on for yourself. These are the words that others call you by, the doctor's office or school knows, the government lists you under. But what is the symbol for those words, the one that identifies you? It's one you have already created and crafted over time since you first held a pencil: your signature.

From the time I started working in retail in my early teens to now when I ring up sales at art shows on my tablet, I have noticed that the majority of people's signatures are some sort of scribble. The words and their individual letters are often nearly indecipherable. People are more likely to leave a loose swirl or similar grouping of lines, making shapes instead of recognizable letters, to the point where the signature becomes more an idea of the name—of you—than a word. The power of this symbol to the world is that you are acknowledging a transaction or change of some sort when you apply it. The meaning of your signature is your acceptance, approval, or endorsement of an idea. That's the meaning found in that mark.

Your signature also signifies that you know how to wield a pen or stylus or use your finger to draw symbols. If you can develop and draw your own signature, you can create and make sigils! In this chapter we're going to explore how we can relate words with symbols and then create our own system of marks instilled with our own meaning.

The Symbolism That Lives in Lines

A single symbol can have so many meanings—which can change and evolve over time and differ from culture to culture. If we consider the theory that humanity all started in one place, it's possible that we created a set of signs and symbols there first. Then, as we migrated and moved outward into the world, it's only natural that those markings would evolve over time. As our ancestors encountered new landscapes, climates, and animals, the symbol vocabulary grew and changed. It's also wise to keep in mind that information passes and changes from generation to generation for a multitude of reasons. Those differences affect how each culture sees and interprets the world. Some symbols fall out of use and become forgotten, current ones get altered to suit one's needs, and new marks are created.

It's important to keep all of this evolving history in mind when looking at what elements you are going to use in making your sigils. I'm going to introduce you to many of the marks and shapes I use in creating my sigils, and you're probably going to find many of them familiar. Some of them you may have never considered as having meaning, and others you may find you have your own interpretations for, different from my own. There are also most certainly other shapes and symbols I haven't listed here that you may feel inclined to use in your sigils. My job here is twofold: to expose you to new ways of looking at dots, lines, marks, and symbols and to help you think about what is important and meaningful for *you*.

For each mark or shape, I've left room for you to make notes. Feel free to write down your gut reaction to each item as we go over it. We're going to start by looking at the most basic of marks and shapes. Then we'll consider some more complex signs, established symbols, letters, and other pictorial systems for your vocabulary. Next we'll explore how numbers as well as colors come into play when designing sigils. You can make increasingly complex sigils or opt for the simplest possible design. What matters most is answering this question: What works best for you?

Basic Shapes and Signs

We're going to start with the most simple of marks and shapes and build our way up to more complex signs. For each element I have included a name, an illustration, and a suggestion of its meaning, as well as possible applications for it, depending on context and composition. Remember, there's a *lot* of power and meaning to be found in the most basic of marks, so don't rush through or overlook them to get to the more complicated ones.

There are many more symbols that you can use than I have listed here—these are the ones that I find are the most common and universal in usage. I've provided a list of excellent books in the "Bibliography and Suggestions for Further Research" section if you wish to pursue a deeper exploration of symbols.

●

Point (Closed Dot): This is such a simple mark, yet it can hold so much meaning. The point, or closed dot, literally is the beginning of all marks we make. It can be a monad, a seed, a center mark, or an atom—the representation of energy itself. It can be a point of origin, where everything starts, or a point of destination, where something ends. It can represent a stop along the way, a place of rest—consider what the period means at the end of a sentence. It can be grouped with other dots to signify a number, mark a constellation, show a lightly defined trail, or create the feeling of an aura of energy.

_____

_____

_____

_____

Open Dot: Not much bigger in size than the closed dot, the open dot is a tiny empty circle. It can be seen as a point to be achieved, a seed, the smallest possible container, the nucleus of a cell or atom. This symbol talks of possibilities, options to be defined, and choices to be made.

_____

_____

_____

_____

Circle: Larger than the open dot is the circle. Most simply, a circle is a container and can symbolize protection—creating sacred space within it—or it can be a holder to prevent something from getting out. It can represent wholeness, completion, sacredness, purity, or potential. It may also be a sphere, standing in for the sun or the full phase of the moon. It can also represent divinity, as in deity or spirit, or the source of knowledge and commands, referencing the brain or nucleus. Circle variations: with a chevron to represent ouroboros, or with a line across it to indicate "prohibited" or "stop."

_____

_____

_____

_____

Horizontal Line: The horizontal line, traveling east-west, can represent the ground, the baseline, the foundation, or the horizon. It can also be the middle divide—marking the difference between above and below, acting as a border. It can delineate a step or a hurdle to overcome. As a short line, it can be the concept of minus (to subtract or remove). Two short parallel horizontal lines can show the sign for equal or mark equality. Extended parallel lines can represent a canal, channel, chute, or road.

Vertical Line: The vertical line travels north-south, connecting above and below or heaven and earth, or forming a border between left and right spaces. It can represent a phallus (erect or at rest), a tree, a tower, or an elevator. Grouped together, vertical lines can symbolize walls, pillars, or tally marks (especially when crossed with a diagonal line).

Dotted or Dashed Line: A dotted line (a line made up of separated dots) tends to have a more fanciful feeling to it—the path of an animal going about its business, like a bee buzzing from flower to flower, a squirrel collecting nuts, or a child at play. A dashed line (a line made up of minus symbols) tends to have more of a sense of intentional focus or a planned trajectory. Think of the marked lines on a highway or road. The spaces and patterns indicate when it's safe to pass, turn, or leave your lane. Either type of line can be used to connect points or indicate a sense of movement.

path

Diagonal Line: The diagonal line is dynamic, depicting moving energy in an increasing or decreasing fashion. It can also be the path of something rising or falling. The severity of the angle will affect the sense of how quickly or slowly something is moving. The diagonal line can speak to challenges to overcome, or sliding downward smoothly.

_____

_____

_____

_____

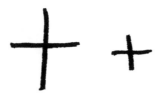

Cross: The cross is a perpendicular intersection of a horizontal and a vertical line. Most simply, it is a meeting place or crossroads, where two different ideas interact. In terms of math, a small cross is a plus sign (addition). In science, it is the symbol for a proton or positive ion, marking energy. If all of the "arms" of the cross are equal, it represents balance.

_____

_____

_____

_____

Chevron: A chevron is a V-shaped mark. Chevrons are most commonly recognized as the "greater than" and "less than" symbols when pointing east or west—and as "up" and "down" buttons when pointing north or south, as well as a mountain or valley. Because they feature a convergence of lines, they can be used for capturing or dispelling energy. Another way to think of chevrons is that they are "open mouths," like an alligator opening its jaws wide to consume something. They combine with other shapes to make many influential symbols such as triangles, stars, and arrows. The chevron is also the Roman numeral for five (see the "Numbers" section later in this chapter).

_____

_____

_____

_____

X: Similar to the cross, the X is an intersection of diagonal lines, which makes for more dynamic/active energy. In maps and myth, X often marks the spot. In basic math, the x can be a symbol for multiplication, while in algebra it's often the variable or unknown value in the equation we're trying to solve. X is also used to mark a place for a signature, or to take the place of one. In a similar vein, X (now more commonly seen as XOXO) has been used to signify a kiss—as in love, or a declaration of truth or loyalty. Yet it can also mark something that is forbidden or prohibited, as well as a hazard—think of the stereotypical moonshine jug with three Xs inscribed on it. It is also the Roman numeral for ten (see the "Numbers" section later in this chapter).

Arrow: Most simply, an arrow is a line with a chevron at one end. The other end could be un-
marked (for continuous energy), end in a point (origin mark) or a parallel chevron (emphasizing
the direction of the first chevron), or meet a perpendicular line at its base (foundation). An arrow
can also have opposing chevrons at each endpoint facing outward, depicting energy shooting in two
directions or a choice of directions. When the chevrons point inward toward the line, the arrow becomes rooted. When the arrow is vertical and paired with two inward-facing chevrons, it can depict
a tree, with the branches reaching upward and the roots going down into the ground. But when this
same arrow is positioned horizontally or diagonally, it becomes evocative of a snake tongue, testing
the air around itself.

_____

_____

_____

_____

Wavy Line: The wavy line gives a feeling of flowing movement. When positioned horizontally, it can represent water (streams, rivers, waves), fluidity, rolling hills, flexibility, snakes or snakelike motion (especially with an inward-pointing chevron head), and vibrations. When in the vertical position, it can symbolize rays of light, divinity, serenity, and vines (growth). The wavy line can also be a thread, as in weaving, sewing, or a spider web. The overall sense of a wavy line is change and transformation.

Zigzag Line: The zigzag line is similar to the wavy line, but its sharp convening lines create a different, more dynamic energy flow—like static versus a hum. It essentially is made up of laterally connected chevrons, giving a feeling of opposition. It can represent snake energy, rays of light, divine touch, and especially lightning. Zigzags also depict rocky or rough terrain, such as a mountain range or a choppy ocean—indicating a dangerous area to overcome.

_____

_____

_____

_____

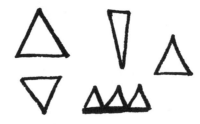

Triangle: The triangle is a closed chevron or, most simply, a contained shape made up of three angles. It can be equal on all sides or be uneven. Most commonly we associate the triangle with the pyramid or mountain, representing a pinnacle or sense of enlightenment and wisdom. The triangle can also represent a tooth or thorn. The longer two of its sides are (even or not), the more the triangle becomes like a dagger, spike, or spearhead. All of these sharp, pointy things give a sense of warning or danger, of being fierce, armed, powerful, or highly protected. The triangle can also be like a sail or an arrowhead, giving a sense of direction or guidance.

Square: The square is two sets of parallel lines overlapping to form an equal-sided box. The square can be a container of holding or can refer to setting aside a specific territory or area to be protected. It can set boundaries from outside influences or bind what's inside of it. The box can be a brick or building block, to signify structure and foundation. Or it could contain mystery or hold secrets, like Pandora's box.

_____

_____

_____

_____

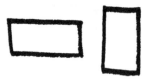

Rectangle: The rectangle has similar properties to the square, its main variation being that its two sets of sides are not equal—one set will be longer. If the two horizontal lines are longer, it could represent a coffin (death or regeneration), a bed (rest, sleep, hidden potential for growth), or money (like a bill). If the vertical lines are longer, it can be a building or tower, a document or contract, a book, or a doorway.

_____

_____

_____

_____

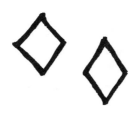

Diamond: The diamond is typically a square set on one of its points instead of resting on its side, or two matching chevrons (or triangles) merged butt to butt. The rotation immediately makes the shape more dynamic and hints at a hidden crossroads at the center of it. The diamond can represent prestige, a goal, a shield, or a financial focus. It can be interpreted as yonic in nature, signify the womb, or represent an entire female form. It can also be a source of light or refraction of light, to magnify the power of something else.

Crescent: A crescent is essentially a half-circle, whether you make a closed form or draw one with a single curved line. Crescents are most commonly associated with lunar energy, especially the waxing and waning phases of the moon. They can also represent divine energy (a god or goddess). A crescent's meaning can change depending on which direction it's facing:

Waxing Crescent: Faces west or left: increasing energy, building up, growing, youth, beginnings

Waning Crescent: Faces east or right: decreasing energy, vanishing, departing, age, cutting (sickle), endings

Upward-Facing Crescent: Facing north: a basket for collecting energy, horns or antlers, a crown, luck (as in an upright horseshoe)

Downward-Facing Crescent: Faces south: draining away, overreaching, or guarding, or a balance of energy when paired with the upward-facing crescent

Spiral: Everyone loves a spiral! It's the shape of life and how things grow—from DNA's helix, to fern fiddleheads and snail shells, to hurricanes and the whorls of galaxies. It's important to note that you can draw a spiral from the outside moving to the center or from a center point moving outward. The spiral symbolizes inspiration and the mythic journey—moving toward the center as well as going away from it, as with labyrinths and mazes. The tail of the spiral can be made to face any direction, which may influence how it flows in your sigil, and can be capped with a chevron—pointing out to direct the energy out of the spiral, or pointing in to pull the energy inward. We can see the modified spiral as energetically slow, like a snail, or fast, like a coiled snake about to spring. Spirals can be used to extend the energy of another symbol as well.

_____

_____

_____

_____

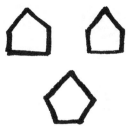

Pentagon: The regular pentagon is a five-sided closed shape with equal sides and interior angles of 108 degrees each. It can be seen as a symbol of power and protection, reminiscent of a shield and a defensive strategy. It is also commonly found in nature—in fruit, flowers, and sea life. An easy way to draw a pentagon is to draw a five-pointed star (see "Pentagram") and connect the points along the outside of the star.

_____

_____

_____

_____

Hexagon: A regular hexagon is a six-sided closed shape with equal sides. Like the spiral and pentagon, it can be found in nature, most notably in the honeycomb of a beehive. The hexagon can represent a tribe, unity, or being part of a group or collective, as well as sweetness (honey), a place to store or hold something, and being industrious.

_____

_____

_____

_____

Other Polygons: I've included these here in case you're wondering about irregular pentagons, hexagons, or any other shape with a number prefix in its name followed by "gon." A polygon is essentially a plane figure with a minimum of three straight sides and angles, and generally has five or more. All of the sides and angles do not have to be equal, and you can have as many sides as you'd like. They can be convex or concave. It's actually very easy to build a polygon inadvertently while crafting a sigil, after layering shapes and lines on top of each other. It could be a happy accident (something that works out well without planning), or you could deliberately build a certain style or number of polygons because of an association with that shape or number. (See the "Numbers" section later in this chapter for suggestions of meanings to consider.)

_____

_____

_____

_____

Star: There are a variety of articulated star shapes you can use in sigils. They all collectively have celestial symbolism, being points of light, balls of energy, something to be guided by—which also brings in the concepts of divinity and sovereignty. All stars made by intersecting lines speak of connecting and interconnectivity, making them excellent symbols of protection and blessing. (See tips on how to draw stars in Chapter 4: Design Guidance.)

Pentagram

The five-pointed star is one of my favorites to use in sigils. The five points can represent the five elements (earth, air, fire, water, and spirit) or the human body (legs, arms, and head). The upright pentagram is an ascending star, while the inverted pentagram is a descending star. When a pentagram alludes to the human body, there are conflicting opinions on which is "masculine" and which is "feminine." I've heard the ascending star called masculine, because the top is pointed, like an erect phallus, which makes the descending star feminine because of the valley. But if you're looking at it like a human being, the top point is the head of the body, making it female. And well, inversely, the descending star may have a large phallus hanging down, but it lacks a head then. So it is really best not to get hung up on equipment—because it's a star. I don't see either direction as negative or positive in terms of good or evil; they're simply kinds of energy. An ascending star can signify heavenly direction, birth, and creating energy. Inversely, the descending star can represent energy moving to the underworld, death, and rebirth. You can also draw them pointing left/east or right/west if you wish to push energy in that direction.

Hexagram

Most commonly recognized as the Star of David in the Jewish faith (though it does show up in other cultures), the hexagram is formed by two overlapping equilateral triangles—or a hexagon adorned with a smaller triangle pointing out from each of its sides. Whereas the pentagram has a "head" that directs it, the hexagram points equally in all directions. It is the perfect union of above and below, or left and right, depending on how you draw it. It has a feeling of all gender/non-binary structure to it.

Septagram

As its name implies, this star has seven points and is found in many diverse traditions that hold the number seven to be sacred, from Faery paths, alchemy, and Thelema to Christianity and Native American beliefs. It embodies magical power, wards off evil, and can symbolize the seven days of the week, creation, etc.

Asterisk

The asterisk (*) can vary in the number of points it has, depending on the font and cultural reference. The most common asterisk is the six-pointed one, formed by three intersecting lines (one vertical line, plus two diagonals that form an X), and the more densely compact eight-pointed one, formed by four intersecting lines (a perpendicular set, and an X set of diagonals). In theory, you could crisscross as many lines as you'd like; the overall effect will depend on the physical size of the star. Because they are not closed shapes like the other stars, asterisks are the most energetic, bursting outward, adding a sense of sparkle to a design. In language, they call attention to additional details and information and they hide words and letters (such as passwords and expletives). In this context, they symbolize secrets, privacy, and hidden knowledge waiting to be discovered.

_____

_____

_____

_____

Heart: In terms of the body, the heart is the organ through which everything gets filtered, the core of our being. We associate it with love, romance, passion, loyalty, devotion, compassion, and joy. A whole heart is a happy or content heart, whereas a heart that is bisected may be divided, broken, or reforming. An inverted heart can symbolize sadness, but it can also call for introspection, grounding, thoughtfulness, and deeper consideration as it becomes spade-shaped, for digging deep. Two spirals entwined at the bottom and circling toward each other to form an open heart signify partnership and developing relationships, as well as opposites coming together in harmony and balance. Two hearts mirrored at the tip signify the joining of two individuals as one, with a sense of infinite energy circulating between them. Three hearts joined together at the base form a club, representing creativity, responsive action, or a triad of lovers. Four hearts similarly joined give us the shape of the shamrock, a common symbol for good luck and prosperity.

Vesica Piscis or Mandorla: The double-pointed oval, or almond shape, is the basis for several meaningful symbols. Most simply, it is an egg, seed, or nut (*mandorla* is Italian for almond). In many religious paintings, a mandorla frames the figure of a saint, spirit, or god like a halo, signifying their divine essence. In terms of the body, it is the yoni, invoking the vulva/female genitalia, and hence is the gateway to and from the vagina, uterus, ovaries, etc. The mandorla symbolizes entrance into this world, as well as feminine sexuality. Referencing the *vesica piscis*, we get a fish shape if we add a little triangle pointing into one of the oval's points, making a tail. The fish is often associated with Christianity, but in other cultures it represents fertility, fluidity, and the element of water.

_____

_____

_____

_____

Eye: Often found building upon the mandorla shape or sometimes a larger circle with concentric circles, the eye is a powerful symbol. Most obviously, the eye represents physical sight, but it can also represent psychic insight, spiritual wisdom, and intuition (the "third eye" or the Eye of Horus). In the countries that border the Mediterranean Sea, eyes are still painted on the prows of ships to bring added guidance and protection. Also throughout this region we find eye charms used to ward off the "evil eye"—a concept based on the belief that someone's jealous gaze can harm your luck, prosperity, or fertility, even if it isn't intentional. The eye charm then repels or reflects that gaze, protecting and blessing you. It literally is keeping an eye out for you, watching over you. (There are numerous charms used for this purpose, and a lot of fantastic lore, but the eye tends to be the most recognizable one.)

_____

_____

_____

_____

Infinity and Hourglass: The figure eight, whether vertical or horizontal, is the symbol for infinity—an endless, fluid looping of energy. It's an ideal symbol to use when you need to represent both stability and movement. If you flatten the rounded ends of the vertical eight, it becomes an hourglass. Therefore it is a symbol of time, limits, restrictions, rules, guidelines, and learning to balance.

_____

_____

_____

_____

Wheels and Shields: When you overlap an X, perpendicular lines, or an asterisk with an open circle, you get wheels or shields. A separation of four parts can represent earth, air, fire, and water (the quadrants) bound by spirit (the circle). The X in the circle can feel like a target to draw or repel energy, depending on what else is around it (hence a shield). Creating six or eight "spokes" in the center of a circle makes a wheel for movement and change, or a cosmic pizza. (Think about it: sometimes a sigil is all about getting a slice of the pie.)

_____

_____

_____

_____

Wings: The reason for adding wings to any shape is pretty self-explanatory: it adds a sense of flight, swiftness, elevation, lightness, and motion. Wings give the impression that whatever they surround will take off at any moment—and that an idea can soar or rise above. They can also symbolize "in memory of" in the sense of angel wings. Also, birds in many myths hold on to memories (especially ravens), keep or share wisdom (owls), or pass along gossip and news (songbirds).

_____

_____

_____

_____

Key and Keyhole: Keys have a rich symbolic history. They can open doors or lock them to keep others out. They can grant access to another realm, and represent wisdom, maturity, success, and power. In terms of property, they allow access and bestow ownership. Inherently related to the key is the keyhole, the access point for the key. It is a place that is locked and protected, or represents the potential for something to be unlocked and revealed. Looking through it, we may get a peek into another world. The pair can take on sexual connotations, most commonly with the key as the tab and the keyhole as the slot.

_____

_____

_____

_____

Scales: Scales are for weighing and finding balance, to determine the value, worth, or price of something. They also symbolize justice and a call to order. Think of the statue of blind Justice holding her scales, or the scene from the Egyptian Book of the Dead where the deceased's heart is weighed against a feather to see if the individual was a good person in life.

_____

_____

_____

_____

Anchor: The anchor of a boat functions to hold the vessel in place, to prevent it from drifting or getting caught up in the current and becoming lost. Therefore its inherent symbolism is of safety, security, stability, hope, and safe harbor. An anchor can also weigh or slow something down.

_____

_____

_____

_____

Butterfly: The butterfly most commonly represents transformation, due to its metamorphosis from caterpillar to cocoon to its beautiful adult state. This winged insect can also signify happiness, lightheartedness, and whimsy. In chaos theory there is a concept known as the butterfly effect—the idea that one small, seemingly insignificant action can cause a large-scale chain reaction.

_____

_____

_____

_____

Hand: Going all the way back to our cave-painting ancestors, the hand finds significance in every culture. We've long recognized its usefulness and ability to transfer power. When I incorporate a hand into a sigil, it's most often the stylized symbol known as the *hamsa, khamsa,* or *Hand of Fatima* (or Mary). This is an open palm shape with the fingers together, and it protects, guides, blesses, and brings luck, happiness, and health. Other favorite hand shapes include the *mano cornuto* (sign of the horns) and the *mano figa* (fig hand), both of which ward off the evil eye but are more difficult to draw for a sigil. It's best to keep sigils simple and linear.

_____

_____

_____

_____

Spoon: While there are certainly classic associations for the spoon, I'm more interested in this one as an important modern symbol for our current society. The spoon theory is a metaphor that explains how someone living with a disability or chronic illness (often "invisible" since their illness may not be visibly apparent) has a limited amount of energy available for the regular activities of daily living and other tasks. Every activity requires a certain amount of "spoons." Someone with one of these conditions who runs out of spoons must rest and recharge until their spoons are replenished. Therefore, the spoon can be a very important part of a sigil for someone fighting a chronic illness.

_____

_____

_____

_____

Standard

Modified

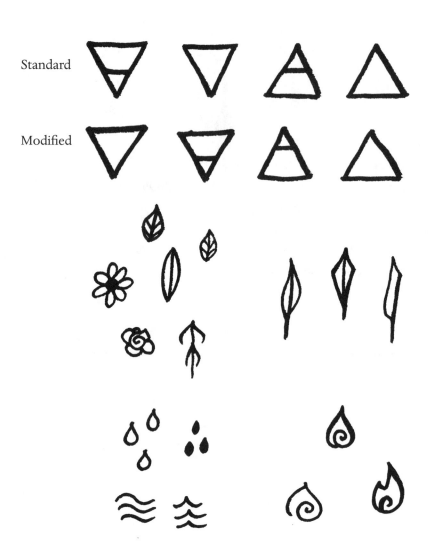

ELEMENTS

Sometimes you will want to represent an element or elements in your sigil. Two good options are pictographs and alchemical symbols. The pictograph version is the most intuitive, connecting each element with a shape or symbol that you probably already associate it with. Here are some pictograph examples:

Earth: leaf or flower

Air: feather or clouds

Fire: flame

Water: droplets or waves

The alchemical versions take a little more getting used to—all of the elements are represented by upright or inverted triangles, with or without horizontal lines in them. I have included here the traditional set of symbols (earth, water, air, fire) as well as a modified version I came across in recent years. The modified version is almost identical to the traditional one, with the exception of earth and water being switched. I prefer it because it makes a little more sense to me. Why? Well, it feels to me that air and water, with their horizontal lines, show their capacity to fill spaces in fluid ways. Fire is all-consuming, and earth is typically solid, so their lack of lines reflects their absolute nature.

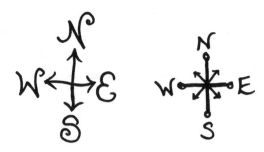

DIRECTIONS

You may find it useful to reference the cardinal directions in your sigils. One option is to use a compass rose as a symbol for finding purpose or placement. Or you could choose to focus on a specific direction in regard to physical movement. Another way of considering direction is not in terms of using a letter to mark a direction (N, S, E, W) but rather how you place other marks in your sigil to represent direction-based correspondences. Do you need something to move to the east or stop in the west? Then use a symbol (like an arrow or an X) in that corresponding location on your sigil to aid your work. Here is a handy list of meanings we use in the Modern Tradition:

North: earth, but also sky, upward motion, taking root for future potential growth

East: air, right, moving toward the future, new direction

South: fire, passion, returning to the ground/basics, renewal, sensual, sexual

West: water, fluidity, to the past or coming from it, memory, dream, cleansing, immersion

_____

_____

_____

_____

NUMBERS

There are several ways you can incorporate numbers into your sigils. I've listed meanings for the most commonly used numbers (0–12) as well as 13, 21, and 42. If there is a certain number I haven't listed that is meaningful for you—a birthday, an age, etc.—then by all means use it. One way is to incorporate the number itself as a symbol, using either the standard form of the number or the Roman numeral (or any way you prefer to draw numbers). Or you can use shapes repeated in a motif to represent a number, such as five dots, a single star, or ten lines. Also, don't feel like you have to draw forty-two marks on a line. You can have seven six-pointed stars instead.

Zero (0): pure, potential, clean, possibility, void, empty

One (1, I): beginning, solidarity, single, prime, goal, self

Two (2, II): duality, pairings, balance, compassion, equality, exchange

Three (3, III): trinity, divine, trident, giving, blessing, past/present/future, fate

Four (4, IV): balance, quarters, grounding, foundation, seeking roots, home

Five (5, V): cycles, blessing, protection, family, guidance

Six (6, VI): journey, movement, memory, passion, love, luck, 3 + 3

Seven (7, VII): activation, action, sacredness, force, mystery, dreams

Eight (8, VIII): achievement, infinity, strength, wisdom, success, wealth

Nine (9, IX): doorway to completion, reflection, introspection, 3 × 3 and 3 + 3 + 3

Ten (10, X): completion of a cycle, wheel, wholeness

Eleven (11, XI): balance, twins, justice, combined strength

Twelve (12, XII): preparation, waiting, introspection, a year, sets, tribes/tribal

Thirteen (13, XIII): sacred, death, rebirth, lunar energy

Twenty-One (21, XXI): universal, 7×3, luck, success

Forty-Two (42, XXXXII): Answer to the Ultimate Question of Life, the Universe, and Everything, or 6×7

ZODIAC AND ASTROLOGICAL SIGNS

Sometimes you may want to reference a particular person's energy, and an easy way to do that is to use the symbol for their astrological sign. I'm not huge into astrology, but when I give tarot readings I often ask the client what their zodiac sign is. It typically gives me an inside look into their personality so I can then deliver the best advice for what comes up in the cards. Why? Because I have found that various signs tend to have different physical, mental, and emotional approaches to problems and issues. Some people also identify very strongly with their sign as a way to explain themselves, and using the symbol in a sigil can help focus on the best attributes of the sign.

In addition to the astrological sign associated with each zodiac symbol, there's also the star constellation for each sign. That can be a more subtle way of incorporating the sign into a sigil, or one that you may find more meaningful. And while we're considering the sky, there are also the symbols for the planets that are used in astrology. We already covered simple symbols that can represent other heavenly bodies, so it's not much more of a stretch to consider the planets. So again, if that's something you resonate with, then why not incorporate one of those symbols if it works for your goal?

It's also helpful to note that the twelve signs are also aligned with the elements. Aquarius, Gemini, and Libra are air signs. Pisces, Cancer, and Scorpio are water signs. Aries, Leo, and Sagittarius are of fire. And last but not least, the earth signs are Taurus, Virgo, and Capricorn.

_____

_____

_____

_____

LETTERS

Letters are another option for symbols that you can use in your sigils. To avoid confusion, I would like to point something out about the method of sigil making that I described in the introduction. It's a popular method developed by chaos magic folks, and it involves focusing your intent into a sentence and writing it down. Next you strike out all of the vowels to prevent your brain from creating word associations, and remove duplicate consonants. Then from there you build a design out of the remaining consonants to make your sigil. This is definitely one way to do it. But that's not how we'll be doing sigil witchery, and more specifically, this is not what I'm referring to in this section.

For starters, I don't have anything against vowels, nor do I have a preference for consonants. In fact, the chanting of vowel sounds is a handy way to attune and commune with deities and spirits in many paths. Nor do I think it's especially helpful to disassociate from the words in order to trigger your right brain. As you'll see in the next chapter, we'll be using those words to develop connections to images that will help remind us of our goals.

The main idea here is that you could include letters in your sigil in the form of initials to represent a person or the name of an idea. Consider the use of monograms and name jewelry, for example. They signify ownership and identity. When signing important forms, there are often sections where we must initial on the line to indicate "I have read and understand this part" versus using our full signature. Using somewhat recognizable initials in your sigil is especially helpful if you're creating one that is meant to be a kind of logo or identifying mark. Lastly, if you're going to use initials, pull the letters from the language you know best, rather than picking something out because it looks cool. Why add another layer of translation when you can be direct?

COLORS

What color you draw your sigil in isn't a huge deal. Just use whatever pen and paper you can find that will work for what you need, such as a piece of chalk for something that will be washed away, or a black Sharpie to put a hidden mark on your desk chair. But if you like adding additional associations *and* you have the time and resources to get fancy, here is a list of colors and their possible meanings to whet your appetite. You can make certain elements of your sigil different colors, or make it all one color. Remember, you may respond to a color in a different way from what I have listed here, so always go with your gut. These are only suggestions.

Red: blood, fire, anger, passion, love, good luck, fertility, stop

Orange: devotion, happiness, warmth, friendship

Yellow: light, air, warning, alert, pause, slow down

Green: life, hope, joy, fertility, growth, ecology, money

Blue: water, sky, calm, wisdom, purification

Purple: loyalty, justice, wealth, bravery, royalty   * *intuition*

Pink: love, romance, fertility, tenderness, children

Brown: earth, humility, potential, returning

White: purity, divinity, spirit, death, full moon

Black: underworld, mystery, wholeness, new moon

Silver: lunar, divinity, spirit, psychic power

Gold: solar, divinity, spirit, physical power

_____

_____

_____

_____

OTHER SYMBOL SYSTEMS

This would be the part of the book where some of you might say, *That's cool, but where are the runes? What about Icelandic magic or Chinese characters? How about those Aboriginal or Berber markings you showed us in the first section?* If you practice any of those paths or originate from them, then you should already have reference guides for knowing and using those symbols. If you don't, then be prepared to do some serious research before incorporating those symbols into your work.

My goal in this chapter has been to focus on common symbols found across many cultures that a wide variety of practitioners can identify with. I'm not a fan of using something just because it looks cool. You should understand what a symbol means, where it comes from, and how and why it's used. This also goes for other magical alphabets such as Enochian, Theban, and Ogham. There's the argument for secrecy, but you're not writing a thesis here for others to read, you're making a sigil.

If you have a solid familiarity with a magical alphabet or symbol system, that typically means two things: (1) you respect and have a good relationship with it, and (2) when you see one of those symbols, it immediately generates that meaning in your head. It's very important in sigil witchery to have the most direct line of communication between the left and right sides of your brain. If you see another alphabet and have to translate it in your head to another language and then send the meaning back again to the other side of your brain to form a picture, that's a lot of extra work for the sake of looking cool.

It doesn't make you a better Witch or up your resumé to use alphabets and systems that don't feel intrinsic to you. For example, I think the Runic alphabets look and are incredible, but I've never felt the pull to go deeper. Despite coming from a long line of people who liked to sleep with people from other cultures, I don't have a family connection to that area. Long ago, when I was but a young Witchlet, the runes and I had a conversation that went like this: "It's nice to meet you, but nope, this isn't going to work out. Have a nice day."

Now on the other hand, tarot has always come naturally to me. I'm deeply fascinated with the multitude of systems and continue to study them. I often refer back to the tarot for numerical associations as well as other symbolic meanings. So if you do feel a pull toward a system or alphabet, then go ahead and take the time to study it. Become familiar with it, and then it will make far more sense to use it, as it becomes a part of you.

Another question you might ask at this point is this: *I'm a (whatever your trade/hobby is). Is it okay if I incorporate (related system) into my sigils?* The answer is yes! If you're a musician, then I think using musical notation makes perfect sense. If you're a dancer and you have specific shapes that you use in notating choreography, then that has symbolic meaning for you. If you're an engineer, then it could be symbols from equations. If you find additional meaning in these marks, then it makes sense to use them, as long as they help the process.

Finding Symbolism in Words: Building a Symbol Library

We've gone through a lot of common shapes, signs, and symbols, with their suggested interpretations. The next step is to consider what symbols *you* associate with the words you might use to create a sigil. For some people, this symbol-word association will come easily. For others, it may take a bit of practice. But on some level *everyone* has an image they associate with a word. The trick is to move out of a traditional, representational image into a simplified symbol.

For example, let's look at the word *community*. A community is a group of people, usually with something in common—an idea, place, or trait that brings them together. For some people, the shape they may associate with the word community is a circle—referring to a circle of friends, a protective group, or a spiritual gathering. For others, they may see it as a square—in the sense of a foundation or building block. Still others may see it as a triangle, referencing a steeple, an organization, or a balance between different viewpoints. Someone else may visualize community as a collection of dots arranged in a hexagon—representing individuals coming together to form a loose collective or hive. All of these associations are correct, so it's important to take the time to figure out what feels right for you.

What about verbs? They have associations just like nouns. Consider the word *growth*. An image of growth could be a straight, upward-facing arrow emerging out of a dot. Or maybe you're thinking of organic growth (in terms of time and experience), so perhaps the shaft of the arrow will be wavy. Maybe it's a vertical line accompanied by chevrons (ends pointing up), ending in an upright-pointing star. Or you could use a mandorla coming off a vertical line to represent a leaf shape.

To help prepare you for the next chapter, I've included a list of words that are commonly found in sigil work. Look them over and take the time to consider how you would translate each word into a symbol. The purpose of this practice is not to create a dictionary of word-symbol relationships that will be set in stone. Words do change over time and vary according to the situation, but it's good to encourage your brain to connect words and images. Then put your ideas down on paper—you'll see why this is important in the next chapter. This practice will definitely aid you in many magical practices—not just sigil witchery!

Feel free to add other words to this list or use synonyms for ones provided that resonate more with you. There is no harm in building up a reference list of words and symbols to guide you. Just make sure that it's your own, and that you get comfortable with naturally associating shapes and words in your head over time.

Your Word-Symbol Associations			
Word	*Symbol*	*Word*	*Symbol*
Acquire		Align	
Art		Balance	
Banish		Blessing	
Change		Cleanse	
Community		Create	

Your Word-Symbol Associations			
Word	*Symbol*	*Word*	*Symbol*
Decrease		Dream	
Emerge		Family	
Fertility		Friendship	
Give		Grow	
Guide		Happiness	

Your Word-Symbol Associations			
Word	*Symbol*	*Word*	*Symbol*
Healing		Health	
Home		Ignore	
Increase		Inspiration	
Invoke		Journey	
Love		Luck	

Your Word-Symbol Associations			
Word	*Symbol*	*Word*	*Symbol*
Manage		Money	
Mirror		Negotiate	
Overcome		Power	
Prosperity		Remove	
Restrict		Romance	

Your Word-Symbol Associations			
Word	*Symbol*	*Word*	*Symbol*
Solve		Strengthen	
Study		Success	
Sustain		Time	
Trust		Work	

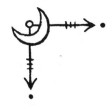

CHAPTER 3
MAKING MAGICK

I think one of the best ways to think about sigil witchery is that it's essentially condensed spellcraft. It doesn't require a lot of space, special supplies, herbal knowledge, or a metaphysical degree. All you need to make a sigil is a surface (something to write on), a writing implement, and the ability to focus on a goal or desired outcome. Have a few minutes, a ballpoint pen, and a sticky note? You're golden!

Of course, you *can* get much more elaborate if you want to. Want to make handmade paper infused with special herbs processed during a certain phase of the moon? Go for it! Want to milk your own squid, liquefy some dragon's blood resin, and conjure up your own ink? Then by all means do it! Basically you can make sigil witchery as simple or as complex as your heart desires.

In order to figure out what will work best for you, let's investigate how and why sigil witchery works, metaphysically and physically. We'll explore the uses, go step by step through the creation process, and consider the large variety of options available to you for implementing your sigils.

UNDERSTANDING MAGICK AND SPELLCRAFT

Magick is the art of focusing your will or intent in order to bring about change in yourself and influence your environment/the world around you.

If that description of magick seems extraordinary, consider what you're doing right this moment—reading. The ability to read this book involves a transfer of energy through cells, nerves, and muscles, all while the rest of your body is going about its business. You understand the letters, form the words, see the sentences, and create the structure in your mind. It goes beyond visual recognition to be stored as memory for you to call upon again in the future. It's technically an "invisible" transfer, but it happens anyway. We constantly influence ourselves and others through our thoughts, emotions, and actions. How does your favorite cat or dog know when you're sad? They can pick up on the subtle signals you put out, even if you're not displaying obvious signs of distress.

Magick and spellcraft function in a very similar way. An idea becomes thought, which becomes action—intentional as well as subconscious—setting things in motion. We can stimulate our senses by burning colorful candles, crushing herbs, anointing with oils, burning incense, choosing certain phases of the moon, framing images, writing words, playing music—all symbols we respond to and coordinate with the goals of our intentions. Still seems farfetched to you? Consider a place where you feel relaxed, perhaps a spa where there is soothing music playing, the floors are warm and comfortable, the air smells of fresh lavender, and the light is soft and atmospheric. All these things have a calming effect on both your brain and your body. Similarly, stress—while often designated as a mental strain—can manifest really harmful effects on your body, including high blood pressure, hair loss, skin irritations, and lowered immune response. But stress is invisible, just "in your head," right? The very real and physical symptoms speak volumes about what our brains can do to our bodies.

So hopefully that explains magick a bit more practically for you. Unless you're living in a Harry Potter film, you can't wave a wand, say some words, and expect fantastic CGI effects to instantly happen. But you *can* focus your will and change patterns of energy within and around you, like how a thread interconnects with other threads in the weaving of fabric.

If we accept and understand that magick is intent put in motion, then spellcraft is the art of arranging the physical to affect the metaphysical. It can be the chanting of a certain rhyme to change the weather, the gathering and burning of herbs with aligning magical correspondences to cleanse a room, or the making of a poppet to heal a person. For our purposes, we're looking specifically at how sigils can be used as spellcraft. That means that sigil witchery is creating and using specific symbols to influence a person, situation, or environment. The act of drawing the shape, recognizing the symbolism found within that sigil, and deciding what to do with it afterward will all play into how we make sigil magick.

By the way, if you're wondering about that *k*, I tend to use this specific spelling of magick when discussing metaphysics with a familiar audience. There are all sorts of debates about the origin and appropriate use of this spelling, with the simplest being the appeal of using an older spelling of the word and distinguishing it from illusion-based stage magic. Frankly I'm not a huge fan of the word with *or* without the *k*, as I think it falls flat in describing the process. It conjures up fantasy when we're dealing with a very real and effective use of energy. But until I find or create a better word, magick will have to do. (If the *k* gives you hives, take an allergy pill and move onward to focus on more important things.)

How Does Drawing Sigils Work?

If you understand that colored candles, herbs, oils, and poppets all work in terms of stimulating the senses through sympathetic magick (like things corresponding to like things, or the part affecting the whole), you may be wondering how just drawing sigils can be effective. All sigils correlate to two *very* important basic things: sight and touch. Sight would be your eye recognizing the shape and its assigned meaning. Then there is the tactile sensation of making the drawing itself, connecting your eye, hand, and brain in a loop of physical and thoughtful recognition.

How important is it that you hand-draw your sigil? *Very.* Multiple studies on memory have shown that people who make physical notes with pen and paper versus typing them remember more.[11] Why? It turns out that our brain uses a different kind of cognitive processing when we write versus when we

---

11. Cindi May, "A Learning Secret: Don't Take Notes with a Laptop," *Scientific American*, June 3, 2014, www.scientificamerican .com/article/a-learning-secret-don-t-take-notes-with-a-laptop.

type. When we listen and type, we are in transcription mode—transcribing audiovisual content without thinking cognitively about it much. Drawing and notetaking by hand takes more time, so you're more actively processing and condensing the information you're seeing and/or hearing. Your brain is far more engaged and involved in the whole process, so you will remember it much better.

Photo of the Artist at Work

Furthermore: "When we write something down, research suggests that as far as our brain is concerned, it's as if we were doing that thing. Writing seems to act as a kind of mini-rehearsal for doing. ... Visualizing doing something can 'trick' the brain into thinking it's actually doing it, and writing something down seems to use enough of the brain to trigger this effect."[12]

So in the process of crafting a sigil, you are accessing the higher cognitive thinking centers in your brain. You're clarifying and editing down information in order to remember the most important parts. You have engaged your brain in such a way that it's already preparing for and visualizing that magick taking effect. The right side of our brain revels in images, so sigils align with the most intuitive and instinctual part of ourselves. It's far easier to manifest something when you can picture it, instantly and subconsciously coordinating it with meaning. The sigil helps create the feeling that what you're looking at engages with all of your being. Pretty impressive for some squiggly lines, eh?

After you've taken the time to create the sigil, you then apply it. Some people talk about "activating" it after you have drawn it. I believe the sigil already becomes activated in the process of making and finalizing it as a drawing. Your brain and being know it's a thing from the experience of creating it. The next step is applying and acknowledging it. Application refers to how you will use it to help you accomplish your goal. Acknowledgment is renewing your association with the sigil. These actions are determined by what you're planning to use your sigil for.

USES FOR SIGIL WITCHERY

Essentially, whatever you can think of to do in regular spellcraft, you can do with sigils—and possibly more! Healing, banishing, binding, unbinding, cleansing, attracting, protecting, fertility, prosperity, love, friendship, partnership, glamour, divination—the list goes on and on. If you can think it, you can draw it.

---

12. Dustin Wax, "Writing and Remembering: Why We Remember What We Write," www.lifehack.org/articles/featured /writing-and-remembering-why-we-remember-what-we-write.html.

In addition to sigils being shorthand for traditional spellwork, they can correspond with ancestors, deities, and other spirits—as our ceremonial magician friends know. But you're not confined to working with that specific set of angels, demons, and other beings, especially if you work in a different culture or system. You can work with your familiar spirits and deities to craft a sigil that's a kind of call sign, mark of familiarity, or symbol of devotion for them.

You can also use a sigil as a mark of ownership (as in, this here thing the sigil is on is *mine*). You can work with a group, tribe, coven, church, or community to design a sigil that represents the organization and its goals. It can be a logo for your business or a personal mark that identifies and describes you as a being. It can even be a family or household crest.

I'm sure that once we go through the creation process and the related application and acknowledgment options, you'll have an even better idea of the multitude of uses for sigil witchery.

STEP BY STEP: HOW TO PLAN AND CREATE YOUR SIGIL

Now that you know the sky's the limit, where to begin? There are four basic steps to sigil creation:

Step 1: Define your goal or identify the problem.

Step 2: Brainstorm a list of what is needed to accomplish that goal or solve the problem.

Step 3: Design the sigil.

Step 4: Apply the sigil, and acknowledge it as necessary.

I'm going to explain in depth the processes behind these four steps. We'll use a practice scenario to illustrate how to work your way through each step. I've included more examples for you in the practical exercises in chapter 5, so you can explore a wider variety of situations and compare possible solutions.

Step 1: Define Your Goal or Identify the Problem

First, consider what it is you wish to accomplish. It's vital to be realistic about the goal, and to take time to consider the possible outcomes, consequences, and ramifications. I have always told my students, "Magick takes the path of least resistance." There is many a myth in world folklore that involves poorly thought-out wishes and the problems they cause. It's better to model your thinking on the savvy mythic figures who exercise foresight and critical thinking. If you just follow your desires and impulses without thinking it through, you will probably not be satisfied or pleased with the result. All actions will lead to a variety of reactions—intended and unintended, positive and negative—so you need to think several steps ahead and be responsible. Being responsible means acknowledging that Witchcraft is more about having power over yourself and your environment than over others. Here are some examples:

Example 1

Good Goal: To be in a romantic relationship that is healthy and happy

Bad Idea: Make Pat fall in love with me

The former allows for options and a better outcome. What if Pat turns out to be a total jerk? Then you're stuck with getting rid of Pat.

Example 2

Good Goal: Being financially secure, stable, and successful, with an income of at least $42,000 a year

Bad Idea: Getting a job or getting a raise at my job

The former focuses on a larger cycle and a specific goal. The latter may not provide you with the money you need for financial stability or provide the environment you need or want. Maybe what you need is a different job.

Example 3

Good Goal: Owning the right home for us that is safe, at or under our goal price, and what my family needs within the next six months in Sky County

Bad Idea: Making sure we get that one house we put a bid on at 303 Happy Place

The former gives a set timeline, financial limit, and area and covers your needs and expectations. That one house you saw may not be best for your needs. It may cost more, have hidden issues, or put you out of the running for a more ideal home.

Example 4

Good Goal: Bring justice and healing for my friend Donna safely and quickly

Bad Idea: May that asshole who hurt Donna burn in a fire.

The former directly helps your friend and sets justice in motion without making how it happens your specific problem. The latter might seem like it brings justice, but it could involve other people getting hurt and doesn't lend energy to helping Donna overcome what happened.

You can see some places above where it's good to be specific and others where it's better to set guidelines without getting too bogged down in details. I'm not going to lecture you on karma, a threefold law of return, or the good/evil coin. Each of us has our own perspective and set of ethics and beliefs. My only recommendation in the moral department is to be thoughtful, consider both the short- and long-term effects, be prepared to take responsibility for your actions, and be careful not to overexert or overextend yourself. Also, don't be a jerk.

Step 2: Brainstorm a List of What Is Needed to Accomplish That Goal or Solve the Problem
Once you have considered step 1, write down what you have come up with in whatever way helps you to process and explain it to yourself. If you're facing a particular problem, you could make a list of the issues and what things may be needed to create a solution. From there, focus on making a list

of key words that summarize what you want to achieve. These words in turn will translate into the shapes and marks you will use to create the sigil. I recommend having at least three to four words to focus on, but not more than, say, ten to twelve.

Let's take one of our "good goals" examples to use as our practice scenario:

Good Goal: Bring justice and healing for my friend Donna safely and quickly

Our key words here are:

justice | healing | Donna | safely | quickly

Step 3: Design the Sigil

Look at your list of words. What shapes, marks, or symbols do you connect with each of them? Here's how I would go about it. Normally this all happens in my head, but for the format of this book, I'll list it for you:

justice: the scales

healing: a heart, spiral energy

Donna: she's a Cancer, so I could use that symbol for her, or a *D* for her name

safely: plus sign, upward crescent

quickly: arrow energy, all directions

At the center of all this is Donna, so I'm going to put the symbol for her down first. I want her to be protected and to focus on healing in a safe place, so I'm going to draw a heart around her symbol, with spirals curling out of the bottom of the heart. Next I'm thinking about "justice" and "safely," so I'm going to place a plus sign coming out of the top of the heart, and build the scales coming out and down from either side of the heart. The top of the plus sign feels empty to me, so I'm going to place the horned crescent on top. That leaves "quickly," so I'm going to draw arrows going out in the cardinal directions. Voilà! A sigil!

Donna's Sigil

Step 4: Apply the Sigil, and Acknowledge It as Necessary

Once you have designed your sigil, it's time to do something with it. What you do with the sigil depends on its purpose. This process is what I call the application of the sigil. Acknowledgment is what you (or the end user) may do *after* the sigil is applied to remember the sigil, reenergize it, or otherwise interact with it.

Some people are really keen on burning their sigils to "activate" them. I tend to look at burning in magick as a means of banishing, cleansing, or otherwise removing or releasing something, which makes burning a sigil rather ineffective if it's not associated with any of those actions. There is a particular school of thought that strongly recommends destroying the sigil after you've created it. The reasoning is that in order for the sigil to work, you must forget it, thereby letting the sigil slide back into your subconscious or unconscious mind. That process dictates that the sigil will not work if you're hyperfocused on its success. That may be a good solution if you tend to get fixated on certain things, but I think it's overkill for most people, especially for those who are adept in metaphysics and familiar with exercising control over their mind and thoughts.

Even if the sigil is often within your field of vision (on your desk, tattooed on your arm, on your mirror, etc.), it falls into the subliminal range of observation—meaning your eyes often look at it without you actually being aware that you're seeing it and consciously thinking about it. This subtle exposure to symbols can make for some pretty effective workings, considering that's the same way a lot of advertising works! (If you see something enough times, you become familiar with it even if you're not aware of it.) Basically, there are a lot of other options for applying and acknowledging your sigil (besides destroying your sigil immediately after designing it) that give you more bang for your buck. We'll cover them extensively in the next section.

Let's return to our practice-scenario sigil for Donna and look at a few different possibilities for application and acknowledgment.

Scenario 1: Donna requested that you make this sigil for her. She's planning to get it tattooed over the spot where she was injured. After it's healed, she plans to anoint it daily with a special essential oil blend made with herbs that focus on healing and justice.

Scenario 2: Donna didn't ask for a sigil, but you wanted to do something for her. You draw the sigil in blue (her favorite color) and place in on your altar next to an item she gave you, where you see it every day.

Scenario 3: Donna asked for a sigil that she can make into a patch. She's going to sew it inside of her favorite coat that she always wears, so when she goes out, she has the sigil with her. She will see it every time she puts the coat on and will feel protected.

Scenario 4: The sigil needs to be virtually invisible for various reasons. To achieve this invisibility, Donna or a practitioner/friend can paint the sigil with salt water on Donna's front and back doors. It will be reapplied on a regular basis, perhaps on the anniversary of the original incident or at every full moon.

Scenario 5: The sigil will be inscribed onto a piece of jewelry by a mutual friend and given to Donna to wear when she feels like she needs something extra to help her feel physically safe and emotionally supported.

Applying Sigils, or Put a Sigil on It!

Once you've designed your sigil, you have a wide variety of options for its application. I've included a number of ideas for you to consider in the next several sections, but I want to take a moment to remind you that simple and basic works too. All you really need is something to write with and to write on. That's it! You don't need fancy paper or an expensive pen, or a specific time of day or moon phase to get work done. That's the beauty of sigil witchery.

From there you could fold the paper up and keep the sigil in your wallet or tape it to your bathroom mirror where you can see it every morning and night. Maybe you have a jar of intentions you plan to put it in. Maybe it will live on a sticky note on your computer screen in your office. Or perhaps you will draw it out in black permanent marker under your chair. None of these options are particularly fancy or time-intensive, but they are practical and effective nonetheless.

But what if you want to do something a little more elaborate? There's nothing wrong with that, so let's explore some options that may stir your cauldron!

THE RITUAL ARTS, OR I GOT THAT WITCH A RITUAL, WITCHES LOVE RITUAL

Let's say you really want to make more of a permanent object out of your sigil. Scrap paper just won't do it for you. Then you're looking at engaging in more of a physical practice—such as ritually making an item. Ritual is the word we use to describe the actions done to bring meaning, purpose, and order to something. It can be very elaborate or simple, as long as it works for you.

If I'm going to get working on some art, I need to set the environment. There needs to be a hot cup of tea, the right lighting, a proper soundtrack, and everything I need handy. My studio is my sacred space, so it doesn't take much to make it ready. You may wish to light a candle or burn some incense. Or you may feel best when you cast a formal circle, setting up very specific sacred space and calling in a spirit or deity to work with you, then breaking it down once you're all done. It all depends on your own preferences and personality, the space, and the amount of time available.

So let's consider some more involved projects for sigils. All of them require setting aside some time and having some patience, and can be altered depending upon your needs and skills.

Illuminating a Sigil with Traditional Pen and Ink on a Card

Illumination

Illumination is a reference to illuminated manuscripts—historical sacred texts carefully and lovingly illustrated, often with expensive and/or archival materials. There is an inherent sense of both dedication and attention to detail present in the illumination process. You can draw or paint your sigil on parchment or infused paper with fine ink. You can purchase some incredibly beautiful paper from art supply stores, and bless it (misting or anointing with oils, smoking with incense, etc.). Or, if you are so inclined, you can make the paper yourself. You can mix herbs into the fibers, and even press and dry it on specific days or during specific moon cycles. You can invest in beautiful India inks in a variety of colors, walnut ink (a lovely sepia tone archival ink), or metallic inks, or you can learn how to make and mix ink for yourself. Once you have all of your supplies handy, you can sit down in your ritual setting and put all of your focus into making the sigil as elaborate and ornate as you wish.

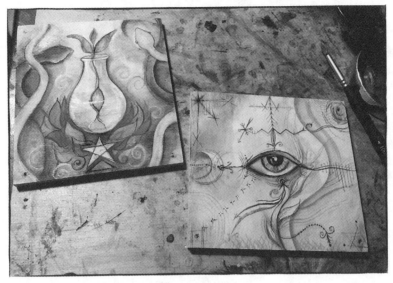

Vitality and *Vision* Spell Paintings by the Author

Painting

I often incorporate sigils into my paintings as part of the artwork, but you can make a painting of a sigil by itself. If you want to make something that's sturdy, durable, and easy to hang, look for ready-made canvases on stretchers or wooden panels. If you're going for a significant size (more than a few inches), steer clear of canvas boards, as they warp over time. I personally don't care for the texture of the canvas getting in the way of my line work, so I prefer wooden panels, but choose what works for you and your budget. Panels and canvases come in a wide variety of sizes and shapes, so select one that will fit your sigil well. For paint, I like to use Delta Ceramcoat acrylic paint. It's inexpensive (under two dollars a bottle), easy to work with (not thick like most acrylics), and available at a wide variety of craft stores. For brushes, I like to use short-handled ones with soft synthetic bristles, like the University Series by Winsor & Newton. They're economical and long-lasting, as long as you clean them properly. (See the next chapter for more art supply recommendations.)

Sigil Satchels—Canvas Bags Embellished with Washable Paint by the Author

Fabric Paint

I'm a fan of fabric paint. (Yes, they still make it, in case you only remember it from the late eighties or early nineties.) It comes in a huge variety of colors, is completely washable, and dries relatively quickly. I like Tulip brand paint. Their 1.25 fluid ounce paint is easy to hold and control, and they make some nice metallics. If you're scared of freehand-drawing your sigil with a little squeeze bottle of paint, you can use chalk or a washable pen/marker/pencil to draw your sigil first, then use it as a guide to paint your sigil. One interesting place you could put a sigil is on your socks—where you'll be able to see it when you put them on, but it will be covered by shoes otherwise. Or maybe you want to infuse your favorite tie—you can paint the sigil on the reverse side. I suppose you could even paint sigils on your underwear if that inspires you. (Perhaps a handy location for a fertility sigil, if that's your goal? Use caution.)

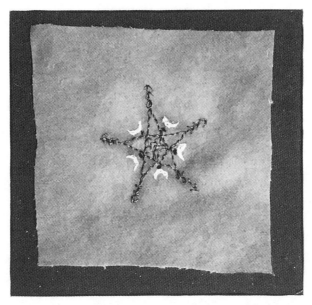

My "Power Sigil" Design, Embroidered and Photographed by Kohenet Ketzirah haMa'agelet

Sewing

Depending on your familiarity with a needle and thread, you can stitch your sigil. You could make a scan of your sigil, figure out how big or small you want it to be, and print it out on a fabric sheet made specifically for your printer. Then cut it out into a patch and sew it wherever you want. I recommend using the printout as a guideline to "draw" with small thread stitches over your sigil's lines. If you're more advanced, you could needlepoint or cross-stitch your sigil, then frame and hang it or make it into a pillow or bag.

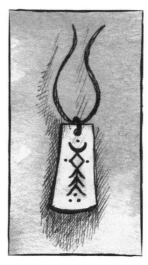

Wood, Bone, and Clay Make Great Bases for Sigil Pendants

Jewelry

Making a sigil into jewelry works for people with a wide variety of skill sets. Many craft and bead stores sell large beads or blank pendants that you can paint, draw, or etch onto. If you live near the ocean or can visit it, sometimes you can find cockleshells or other durable clams that already have a hole drilled in their top by some other animal. The inside is usually very smooth and ideal to paint or draw on. You can coat your painting/drawing with a clear coat of nail polish to protect it. The best part of the shell is that the sigil can be a "secret" on the inside that you wear against your skin. Another jewelry option is to look for a small bottle, vial, or locket. For these, you can draw your sigil on some fine paper, then roll or fold it up to fit in the vessel. If you're an artisan or metalsmith, you could etch or enamel your sigil into metal, glass, bone, clay, wood, etc.—making it into beads, charms, pendants, bracelets, rings, earrings, and so on.

The Vanishing Sigil

Sometimes only you need to know where you put a sigil—no one else needs to know. Or perhaps the sigil is meant to be temporary by design. Here are some ideas for vanishing or invisible sigils.

A Chalk Sigil on a Doorstep

Chalk

Chalk is wonderful because it's cheap, easy to use, and non-toxic to the environment, and it washes away quickly. It's also nearly invisible on other white surfaces. There are several traditions from around the world where the front door area is decorated with chalk designs to bless the house or business and/or appease spirits. The designs are allowed to wash away with the wind, weather, and wear of being walked on, then are reapplied as needed. In many cases, the natural wearing down of the chalk markings carries a sense of sympathetic magick—that the good energy will be recognized and acknowledged as parts of it are carried away by others.

Salt

Using either table salt or sea salt, you can make a "salt" painting out of your sigil, which will eventually be washed, blown, or swept away. If your sigil has to do with purification or cleansing, this is a nice connection. You just don't want to kill or rust out whatever you are sprinkling the salt on. Another way to use salt is to mix a pinch of it into a vessel of water, and then, using a brush, finger, or bound herbs, create a sigil to bless doorways, windows, etc. As long as you keep the salt content low, your marks will be nearly invisible.

Earth

If you need to draw a sigil outside but don't want to use salt or chalk, you could sprinkle sand or dirt, depending on the nature of the ground. Or even more simply, if the ground is loose enough, you could use a stick or your finger to draw your sigil into the earth. With rockier ground, you could align pebbles or small rocks on a path to form the shape of your sigil. With wind, rain, animals, vegetation, and the marks of travel, sigils made of the earth will be dispersed over time.

Earth Sigil

Drawing directly into the earth not only physically connects us to the ground and its elemental properties, but also reminds us that it is the earth we come from and return to. This connection can add meaning to sigils for prosperity and growth, when they are placed in fertile soil, or perhaps to sigils designed to put something to rest, when they are placed on rocky soil, sand, or dry earth. When visiting the ocean, I may draw sigils into the wet sand for the rising tide to take away with its waves—which combines both earth and water elemental concepts.

Water Sigil

Water

As I mentioned with the salt sigil, you can use water to draw sigils for near invisibility. If the surface you're working on is fairly absorbent, you can see the sigil there until it dries. You can bless the water, then draw with it as needed. If you draw a sigil on a steamy window or mirror, then it will vanish, but it will also reappear when that glass gets steamy again—which can be an added bonus for your own house, but no so much if you're drawing it somewhere else. You can also make an herbal infusion with the appropriate herbs, and draw your sigil with that. This can be a good idea for a pillowcase (as long as you give it time to dry before it's slept on) or for blessing a car.

Other possibilities for using water include drawing a sigil on the surface of water—to infuse a drink with it or bless a bath. You could also carve, etch, or mark a sigil onto a piece of ice; as the ice melts, the sigil is released—either into what the ice is placed on or in, or into the air in which the ice/water evaporates.

You can also consider the elemental associations of water as an additional connection. Water is often equated with relationships and emotional considerations (consider the cups suit in the tarot). So if your sigil has to do with balancing or building emotions, or perhaps centers around a romantic or family relationship, you might want to consider water as a possible method of application.

Fire

Sometimes fire *is* what you need. Burning a sigil that was created on paper in a proper container with safety precautions taken can be an effective method for some spellcraft, particularly if you are working with spirits that are associated with smoke and flame. Another possibility is having a sigil that you create for resolution—which is drawn in the ashes of whatever spell you were doing that required things to be burned. That sigil can be a seal to close up and end a situation or redirect any residual energy to a new purpose. You could also draw a sigil out of a material that will burn briefly, and light it on fire (on a safe surface). This can be seen as literally setting an idea on fire.

When considering elemental associations and fire, there are a few different ways of looking at it. I tend to see fire and action as being related, and that carries into the tarot as well for me. Swords are about action, and I relate that to fire, while other people see wands as fire, per the burning inspiration of the mind with ideas. Regardless of which position you take, fire causes active physical change that cannot be undone, and it also provides illumination. If you're looking for drastic change or to shed light on a problem, then applying your sigil with fire may be a good choice.

A Sigil of Smoke

Smoke and Air

Probably the most invisible *and* simplest method is to trace your sigil in the air—with your index finger, a wand, an athame, a crystal, a stick, etc. You could also light an incense stick or a bundle of herbs designed for smoking, using that to draw your sigil with the resulting smoke. Ideally you would select an incense fragrance or collection of herbs that correlate with the intention behind your sigil. I'm not a fan of smoking cigarettes or cigars, but there are some spiritual traditions where using either of these would make perfect sense for drawing your smoke sigil. Regardless of what you set ablaze smoking, be conscious of smoke alarms and not hitting other people or pets with secondhand smoke.

As mentioned in the previous "Fire" section, some people associate swords with the element of air, whereas to me, air represents the very nature of ideas. Ideas are invisible until we act upon them, just as we don't see the wind blowing unless we can notice the trees moving or feel it upon our skin. Air is also necessary for fire to exist, so ideas feed into action. Sigils that are meant to provoke new ideas, generate new patterns, and cause subtle shifts might be best drawn with air or smoke.

Herbs

Most dried herbs come fairly ground-up, so you can siphon them out of a paper cone to sprinkle into the shape of your sigil. If you're doing this outside, let the elements do their thing after you're done. If you're doing this inside, make sure you're not sprinkling anything that's poisonous to pets or children, and be sure you can vacuum it up or sweep it away. You could also ground the herbs up finer, add some water, and make it into a paste that can be dispensed out of a piping bag (like for baking) for added control. This can make it easier to draw the sigil, which will then dry, break down, and vanish outside.

You should use herbs that relate to the purpose of your sigil. For example, you could use lavender for a healing or calming sigil, rosemary for a retaining memory sigil, valerian for a restful sleep sigil, sandalwood for a protection sigil, jasmine for a drawing love sigil, and vervain for an inspiration sigil. Check your favorite herbal witchery book for herbs whose correspondences align with your sigil.

Planting a Sigil

Plant a Sigil

This is a pretty straightforward method and technically does produce visible results, but unless you're making your sigil the size of a large field with plants that are going to stand out, most people will not notice it. The idea here is to use seeds or seedlings to draw your sigil in the soil, then take care of them so they will take root and grow. As the plants grow, so is your sigil acknowledged. This method of application is best used for long-term goals that you are dedicated to achieving—ideally with you planting on your own land or someplace where you can tend to the plants regularly. It definitely requires an investment in time and effort, so it's not for something you have immediate need for.

You have a variety of options to consider when choosing plants to make your sigil. You could go by the color of their leaves or flowers (following the suggestions in the "Colors" section in chapter 2). You could plant herbs that correlate with the purpose of your sigil (see the "Herbs" section earlier in this chapter). You could also grow plants that produce fruits or vegetables that you can consume or share later (see the "Other Nomlicious Sigils" section later in this chapter).

Another option would be to scatter the seeds somewhere else (in the wild, an open lot, etc.) and let nature take its course. Obviously the mindset behind a one-time method like this is very different from a more permanent one like tending a garden over time, so the sigil's intent/purpose would be a bit more "if the fates allow it." Frankly, this method could also be used for a dissent sigil (something that's meant to start the spread of new ideas or fight the system) spread guerrilla-style. Just be responsible and safety-minded. On that note, don't introduce invasive species of plants—especially just to spite someone or something. Reminder: you often reap what you sow, physically and otherwise.

For the Birds

Birdseed

Want your sigil to take flight *and* take root? Then use birdseed to outline your sigil, and let the birds do the rest! Everybody is happy—including the squirrels and other small mammals. (Okay, it may not make your human neighbors too happy, so take that as you will.)

Other Nomlicious Sigils

Why should the birds and small furry beasts have all of the fun? An amazing way to apply your sigil is to absorb it into your own body through eating it (or drinking it, as I mentioned earlier in the "Water" section). It becomes part of your body and you don't technically see it again. Of course, the sigil you choose to eat or drink should be a positive thing that you are consciously internalizing—either for aiding your physical body or for your mental/spiritual well-being.

So if kitchen witchery is your jam, then there are a multitude of ways you could eat your sigils. They could be made with icing, chocolate sauce, whipped cream, powdered sugar, or cinnamon dust—and, I'm sure, with other non-dessert, savory items as well. The sigil could be visible on the plate as a design, or something that is hidden or cooked away in layers. (Just don't go obsessively sculpting it into your mashed potatoes at the dinner table.) If you're not much of a cook but you can artfully handle a bottle of mustard, ketchup, or other condiment, then you could sigil up that hot dog or sandwich. Sigil, Swiss cheese, and salami sandwich, anyone?

Black on Black

Really, this option is not specific to black only, but refers to the idea that you're making your sigil with something that is the same color as the surface you're drawing on. So drawing with a black permanent marker on the black plastic of your desk or chair is one way to do it. There are brands of oil-based paint markers that come in a variety of colors, so you could color-test them first to see if they will work for whatever you need to draw your sigil on. The idea is that you know the sigil is there, but it's not easy for anyone else to see it. This technique is especially handy in situations where you don't want to be explaining your sigil to anyone or constantly answering, "What's that symbol mean?"

Cleaning and Cleansing

You can incorporate sigils into cleaning tasks, basically doing double-duty. Liquid soap and other kinds of cleaners that you can easily manipulate to make shapes with (like a dusting spray or furniture polish) can be used to draw sigils onto the surface you are cleaning. Use protection sigils on floors and windows, harmony and communication sigils on tables, and productivity or relaxation sigils on chairs. You could also carve a bar of soap with a sigil and wash with it. Choose a scent or herbal blend that enhances your sigil. Bonus points if you make the soap yourself or acquire it from someone who hand-makes soaps.

SIGILS ON SKIN

We have looked at a variety of sigil applications that involve either making a physical item or creating ones that are meant to be temporary or invisible in your environment. Now let's look at a different kind of canvas for your sigil: your body.

The Tattooed Sigil

Sometimes you are compelled to create a sigil that you know you want to be a part of your skin. For many practitioners, tattoos are not just decoration—they have spiritual and sacred meanings, and mark the different parts of our lives. These tattoos are for our own eyes, versus something meant to be displayed as adornment. I'm not being down on that kind of tattoo, but rather am pointing out that a lot of consideration and introspection goes into putting a sigil tattoo on your body.

I currently have three sigil tattoos at the time I am writing this, and it's quite possible I'll have more by the time you're holding this book in your hands. My first sigil tattoo I designed for my sternum. It incorporates some North African symbolism (part of my heritage and the heritage of my mentors at the time who helped me make sure the alignment was correct) and images relevant to Modern Traditional Witchcraft. Its purpose is to protect and guide my heart and strengthen my identity, for at the time it was done, I was going through a very rough part in my life. My second and third sigil tattoos were done together, and are located on the tops of my thighs. The spot was largely inspired by one of my own paintings, so that's the subconscious at work for you. Their purpose is to balance the left and right sides of my brain, and help me to focus on my path.

None of them were done with the initial thought of "I want to get a tattoo—what should it be?" There are plenty of tattoos I have fantasized about getting over the years but haven't had done yet. Rather, these tattoos came about because I got a very firm and clear image that this was something that I *needed* to do. And then they were put into action not long after that idea sprang into my head. They are also designed to be things I am personally committed to for the rest of my life.

Photo of the Author's Leg Tattoos

I've also designed a number of sigils for clients that were destined to be tattoos. Or sometimes a client commissions a sigil because they know they need it, and then afterward they decide to get it tattooed as well. The power sigil I created and released in November 2016 has also been tattooed on quite a few people because it called to them. I believe that in the end, if you feel strongly about having a particular sigil tattoo, then you know your way and your body. It's not very likely going to be a thing you'll regret later on in life.

So as you may have guessed, I'm all for sigil tattoos if it makes sense for you. The concept may seem confusing if you're used to a sigil method that says you're supposed to burn the sigil, but as I pointed it out, that's not always the best course of action anyway.

So if you're thinking about getting a sigil tattoo, here are some things to consider:

- What will the sigil do for you?
- Is this something you definitely want to have on your body forever?
- Where will it go and why?
- Can it be seen, or does it need to be hidden?
- What color should it be?

Tip: When choosing a tattoo artist, be sure to look for someone who does exceptionally clear and clean line work. You want to see consistent and even strong lines, as well as a demonstration of knowledge about how the work will age over time. Otherwise you might end up with blurry or messy lines, sooner or later. Look to see healed examples of their work. Meet with them and see if you feel comfortable with them and their workspace. If it doesn't feel right, then find another artist. There are a fair number of artists out there who understand ritual and spirituality in regard to tattoos—so you definitely want to find one of those!

Henna Sigils

Perhaps you are enamored with the idea of having a sigil on your skin, but you can't or don't want to get tattooed. Then henna is a possibility for you. Henna has been used for centuries to dye skin, hair, fingernails, and fabrics—from North Africa to the Middle East to South Asia—by an extensive variety of traveling cultures and faiths. As those people from those areas have migrated, henna has come with them, and it's developed another layer of artistry of its own. Nowadays, you can find henna artists at street fairs, festivals, conventions, and shops.

Real henna paste is made from the henna plant (*Lawsonia inermis*) and is carefully applied to the skin in designs and patterns. Then when it dries and flakes off, the henna leaves the skin dyed a reddish-orange hue, which can last for several weeks. Henna can also be used to paint on bones, the skins of drums, and other natural fibers. It is typically applied with a cone or needle-less syringe tube to make fine lines and tiny marks, which is great for sigils! But it does take a great deal of practice to get the hang of it. It can be difficult to find good-quality, fresh henna—and you don't know until after the design flakes off whether it was good or not. You also want to avoid "black henna," because it's not made from henna but from non-natural chemicals that can cause severe skin irritation.

If henna is something that interests you, I recommend seeing if there are any artists in your area and then talking to them. They often offer classes and training sessions—and there are even henna conferences where artists get together to talk about their trade.

Makeup Sigils

Maybe you would like to put a sigil on your skin temporarily—maybe just for one night or a week. Then turn to the tool of Goths the world over: the eyeliner pen or pencil. NYX, Wet n Wild, and other commonly found budget makeup lines found in the average drugstore make eyeliner pencils in a wide variety of colors—even metallics! There are even glitter pens and brushes if you need to get your glitter on. The thing about makeup is that is wears off—and if you're putting this somewhere under clothes, you are likely going to stain them as well. I also don't expect people to wander around with glitter sigils on their foreheads at work. But sometimes you want to draw a sigil on you for ritual or another special purpose, but you don't want it on you forever. Then makeup is going to be a viable option that can work well for that temporary need.

Acknowledging Your Sigil

Now that I have given you many ideas to consider for applying your sigil, let's look at some easy ways you can acknowledge your sigil—if that is part of your plan. The purpose of acknowledgment is to reorient yourself with the sigil, so you can stimulate your memory and the magical process. It also infuses the sigil with more energy and intent, renewing or refreshing it.

Visual Recognition

With the simplest version of the sigil, just the mere act of drawing it on paper, of putting it where you will see it on a regular basis, will do the trick. Even if you're not sitting down to explicitly stare at it, it's still in your brain's field of vision. If it's on an article of clothing or a piece of jewelry that you put on, or a painting on your altar—once again, that physical and visual contact triggers the sigil.

Tracing

If you feel you need something more hands-on than that, you could trace your sigil. This can be done invisibly with your finger on a flat surface—seeing the sigil in your mind's eye. Or, with a pen or pencil (or fingertip), you can draw over an existing copy of your sigil, meditating upon it. If you've scanned your sigil or have a digital photograph of it, you could trace it with your finger on the screen of a tablet. If you have a stylus, you could do the same with a tablet or in correlation with your computer screen.

Anointing

For sigils that are on the skin, you can anoint them with essential oils once they are properly healed. Actually, during the healing process, when using the proper ointment or salve that your tattoo artist recommends and clean hands, you are still making that mental hand-eye-sigil connection. You can also use oil to draw your sigil on your body, so that it will be absorbed into the skin. In a similar vein, you could carve the sigil onto a bar of soap that you wash with daily.

Refreshing

If you've done one of those more "invisible" kinds of sigils, and you feel more work is still needed, then you can go back and do it again. This works for house blessings and warding, redrawing the sigil where it's needed. It's basically just like housekeeping: making sure everything is clean, clear, and in working order.

Ingesting

Building upon the refreshing concept, remember those nomlicious sigils? Through the process of eating or drinking the sigil, you can visualize it becoming part of you, entering your bloodstream. You can very much ritualize the process and make a daily reminder out of it. For example, you could bake a batch of cookies and ice them with your sigil design. Then for seven days you could sit down at 7:00 p.m. and eat one of those cookies, savoring the taste and visualizing the effects. You could also score a sigil on a bar of chocolate, and break off a section a little at a time.

DEVOTIONAL SIGILS

Devotional sigils are meant to be a personal connection or a kind of contract between you and a spirit or deity. Some deities have sigils they prefer, and they may reveal those to you—either through a dream or vision or by calling your attention to it in your daily travels. Drawing out their sigil is a form of evocation or invocation, depending on the spirit or divine energy you are working with and your purpose. When used in a ritual context, the sigil can be seen as a kind of gateway or bridge between worlds. It can also be used for communication, protection, and guidance outside of defined ritual settings.

While the other kinds of sigils we've talked about focus on gaining power over yourself and your surroundings, the devotional sigil is best seen as a sharing of power or energy. For some practitioners, this is an act of worship. For Modern Traditional Witches, we see it as a partnership or relationship that flows both ways. We show deities and spirits honor and respect and aid them when we can. In turn, they guide and aid us as well.

If you have been working with a particular deity or spirit and haven't yet developed a sigil you both agree on, you can use the following ritual.

DEVOTIONAL DESIGN RITUAL

Prepare the space you are working in as you would for any ritual that requires creating a sacred sphere of energy. Gather a decent-sized sketchbook and a fresh pen or marker—you don't want something that will break, bleed, or run out easily on you. Set up a central comfortable area for you to draw in, and set a pillow adjacent to you (for your guest). Make sure the lighting is just enough for you to see in—not too bright or too dark. Set up an altar or shrine with items that relate to the spirit or deity you are working with. Make sure it's directly in front of your comfy drawing area. Set a white candle that will last at least an hour between you and the altar. Cast the space, and center yourself in the middle, with your drawing materials close by. Take three deep breaths and light the white candle. Say:

O (name of spirit or deity), come to me
By candlelight and altar still.
Bring your power and your will.
Guide my hand with steady line.
Draw tonight your sigil fine.

You can repeat this up to three times if you feel compelled to do so.

Set your pen to paper, and let your drawing arm become loose and relaxed. Your hand may begin to move to perform automatic writing—let it do its thing, just make sure it stays on the paper. You may start to see shapes in your mind's eye, and be compelled to let your hand trace them out. Both are likely options. Just take your time and don't rush it or try to over-correct or analyze it as it happens. Once you feel you have reached the end, close the sketchbook and express your gratitude and appreciation to the energy you have worked with. Extinguish the candle and clear your space.

I recommend performing this ritual one to two hours before you normally go to bed. Then you can see if you get any more information in your sleep. In the morning, center yourself, open up your sketchbook and consider the drawings, and compare them to anything else you might have seen in your dreams. From there, meditate upon the images and craft the sigil.

Sigils in Motion

Though this is not exactly easy to cover in a book format, I want to talk a little about incorporating sigils into movement. As someone who is also a professional dancer, I wholly believe that incorporating movement into ritual is a powerful way to embody magick. One of my favorite things to teach is how to use very basic movements to make a stronger mind-body-spirit connection and get some amazing results. When you're aware of your entire body, from your toes and heels to the top of your head and out to your fingertips, it's so much easier to be engaged with what you're doing. The human body dancing is also all about making shapes in space. You can draw lines and waves with your hands, arms, and legs, trace circles and figure eights with your hips, and so much more.

With this in mind, you could use part or all of your body (depending on your range of movement) to "draw" your sigil. The easiest way would be to use your hand or arm to trace it into the air in front of you. You can "walk" your sigil—tracing it out in steps either by memory or by drawing it on the ground with chalk or etching it into a sandy beach, then walking it like you would a labyrinth. Just make it big enough to do this easily. Also, if you know when you start designing your sigil that you plan on walking it, then it may be very helpful to consider that during the design process so it's easier to move through. You can think about the different parts of the sigil as you process through them—or better yet, just focus on the overall message as you walk it.

Sigils in Motion

But before you do anything with your body, be sure to be present in it first. That may sound silly or obvious, but it's far too easy to just go through the motions versus actively feeling what you're doing with your body. I have included here an outline of what I cover when I teach this in person. (If you need more visual or audible help, check out my *DecoDance* DVD. I cover this exercise in my points for posture, as well as teach a lot of small and large movements you can use to embody a sigil. It also has an accompanying CD of music to work with. Okay, shameless self-promotional bit over!)

BE PRESENT IN YOUR BODY EXERCISE

To start: if possible, get in a standing position, ideally without shoes on (socks are fine). If you're unable to stand, sitting will work too. You may find it helpful to put on some instrumental music with a slow and steady beat, or one that builds slowly to a speed that's comfortable for you. Most importantly, listen to your body, and don't do anything that feels uncomfortable or hurts.

1) First, take a deep breath and let it out over a count of three to four seconds. Take a second deep breath and let it out over a count of six seconds. Then take a third deep breath, and slowly let it out for a count of about eight seconds.

2) Next focus on your feet. Rock your weight so that you shift from toes to balls to heels and back, slowly and gently. (If you're seated, then flex at your ankles to roll your feet against the floor in the same manner.) Think about the temperature and texture of the floor as you make contact with it.

3) Bring your focus from your feet up to your ankles and calves, slowly shifting, squeezing and releasing the muscles in your calves.

4) Next softly bend and gently straighten your knees, without locking them in either position. Think fluid and rolling, like floating on water over small waves.

5) From your knees, think about the front of your thighs (quads) and your backside (glutes). It often helps to place your hands on these parts of yourself, thinking about how they feel as

you squeeze those muscles. (How many ritual exercises include grabbing hold of your own butt?)

6) Move on up to your hips and make sure your pelvis is in a neutral position—not over-extended to the front or overly tucked up in the back like a duck. You can do this by engaging your lower abdominal muscles (as if someone made a motion to punch you in the stomach and you flinched to protect yourself) or by placing your hand on the base of your spine, fingers pointing down. If your fingers are pointing straight down to the floor, you're pretty close to neutral.

7) Check back in with the rest of your body that we've covered so far—feet, calves, knees, quads, and glutes—then focus on your belly. Take a deep breath in and visualize your navel as a "receiving area"—like an ear that is listening to the world.

8) Then move your focus up to your chest, where your sternum (breastbone) is. Take a deep breath in and visualize projecting out from your chest—seeing it as the "speaking zone" as you exhale. Make sure your shoulders are not hunched forward or pushed too far back. You should be able to get a nice deep breath if they're in the correct position.

9) Now shift your attention from your chest up through the center of your neck to your head, and expand out of the top of your head, thinking of reaching up into the sky. Then breathe in again and send the breath down your spine back to your toes. You should feel a sense of connection from the top of your head all the way down to your feet.

10) Take one more deep breath in and visualize energy moving up from your toes, knees, hips, chest, and out your arms all the way to your fingertips. Allow yourself to reach fully out and up with your arms, being aware of your entire arm—shoulder to elbow to wrist to fingers. Now you are fully in your body and ready to move!

Whether or not you decide to put your sigil into motion, I still recommend doing this exercise. Once you've got the order down, it's something you can do in just a couple minutes, every day. It can be helpful as part of a morning balancing routine to get you moving. Or you can use it at the end of the day before you go to bed to calm your mind. It's a fantastic exercise to practice with a group before doing any sort of group working or ritual.

COMPARING SIGIL METHODS

Before we end this chapter and get into the technical aspects of sigil witchery, I would like to talk a bit about why this method is so effective—not just for me, but for all the other people I have taught it to.

First, sigil witchery is a system I have developed intuitively over the years through the combination of my fine art training and personal practice of Modern Traditional Witchcraft. When you study art history extensively—looking at how, where, and why art has been made by humans all over this planet—you begin to get a sense of why we create and the power that is inherent in art. Then when you study the history and practice of folkloric and mythic Witchcraft in its many forms all over the world, you see similar correlations. We seek to influence ourselves, our society, and the world we live in—to exchange power and energy with it. We have been doing this since we first began looking at life in more abstract ways: wondering why we are here, what is life, what is death, what is the meaning of everything, who made us? That is the lens through which I view both art making and witchery.

That is to say my relationship with sigils developed differently from what's standard for occultists. I've never been into ceremonial magic, and I'm not shy about saying that. However, when studying the development of modern Witchcraft, Wicca, and Neo-Paganism in general, I thoroughly researched the societies and systems that fed into them: Agrippa, alchemy, Blavatsky, Crowley, the Golden Dawn, Freemasonry, and on down the rest of the alphabet. I understand and appreciate them for what they are, but give me folklore, ecstatic practices, and the immediacy of getting my hands dirty with pigments and roots without the extra trappings.

And while I have heard about chaos magic for years, my gut reaction to it is similar to that of ceremonial magic. I can appreciate the theories and sentiments, but a lot of the personalities and pontifications wrapped around them really have turned me off repeatedly. It wasn't until after people started asking me to teach my method of crafting sigils that I had to go look at the more commonly known approaches—mainly those popularized by Peter J. Carroll's and Kenneth Grant's writings based on the work of artist and occultist Austin Osman Spare (AOS). Spare apparently became disillusioned with ceremonial magic and personality occultists after dealing with Crowley—which makes me wonder what he would think of that branch of occultism today. Looking at the history and scope of Spare's art and interests, I think that his own *personal* approach to crafting sigils was probably very much related to mine. His work is extremely organic, layered, and visionary in nature. I have a theory that as he was largely surrounded by wordsmiths and intellectual folks who were not artists, he was asked about how he did what he did. (Oh yay, the dreaded "explain your art" question!) And so I think he developed some instructions that would work better for them and sound more concrete than "I just did what came naturally to me."

In fact, after I had the revelation about Spare's method while writing the first draft of this book, I decided to see if I could find out more about my hunch. It seemed so obvious to me, but maybe I was wrong? I found some quotes taken from Spare's *The Book of Pleasure* referenced online in various places by chaos magicians that seemed counter-intuitive to my theory. Then I got hold of a copy of this book to read in its entirety. It's quite clear to me that it is definitely something a passionate, esoterically inspired artist would pen in his mid-twenties, trying to make his mark on the world. It's steeped in a blend of vague language, mysticism, and ire. (I think AOS was a far better artist than he was a writer.) It's easy to see why there are so many different interpretations of his work, because it's rather convoluted and unclear—*but* the language clears up immensely once he gets down to talking about sigils in the section "Sigils. Belief with Protection": "I will now explain their creation and use; there is no difficulty about it, how pure and clear it all is.[25] Out of love for my foolish devotees I invented it."

BOOM. There it is! Translation: *Sigils are such an easy thing for me to do that I don't even have to think about it. However, I devised a method to try to explain to my buddies how to do it.*

And in the attached note 25, Spare drops the mystical shroud of vague esoteric language and tells it like it is: "By this system, you know exactly what (you believe) your Sigil must relate to. If you used any form stupidly, you might possibly 'conjure up' exactly what you did not want—the mother of insanity, or what always happens then, nothing at all. This being the only system, any result other than by it is accidental. Also you do not have to dress up as a traditional magician, wizard or priest, build expensive temples, obtain virgin parchment, black goat's blood, etc., etc., in fact no theatricals or humbug."

Why he didn't choose to write the rest of the book like he did this note, I don't know. I'd rather have a drink with Austin, author of snarky note 25, than the Austin who penned the rest of the book (which summons the need to have a drink just to offset the headache one gets reading it).

To spare you Spare, I'll summarize my understanding of his writing on sigil crafting. He believed sigils work best by accessing the unconscious mind versus actively fixating on an idea. According to him, sigils are best crafted in trancelike states, in a state of extreme exhaustion, or at the moment of sexual release—all points where the conscious mind lets go and the subconscious, unconscious, or non-active thinking side takes over. He thought it best to "erase" the sigil, so that you aren't constantly thinking about it. I don't believe he was being so literal about erasing the sigil, meaning that you should destroy or burn it. Rather, I think he means to be in a relaxed state and then, once you've done your work, move on as needed. Don't fret, worry, or get too hung up on it.

As a visual artist as well as a performer, the various trance/non-thinking states all make perfect sense to me. The more conscious you are of what you're doing, the more your left brain can inhibit your ability to tap into what you're doing. The left brain analyzes and picks everything apart, while the right brain revels in sensation, looking at the overall picture instead of the tiny parts.

Left Brain versus Right Brain?

Now is the perfect time to look at how the left brain and right brain function. It's not that we have two different brains in our skulls, or that everything is so cut and dried. Rather, the left/right brain concept is a good way to look at patterns of thinking, how we process information and relate to the world around us.

Our left brain analyzes the details. It is the center of language and thinking in words, as well as logic, math, and linear explorations. It loves order and facts. The right brain balances it out by thinking in images and looking at the whole picture. It is the center of imagination and creativity, the expressive nonverbal arts, emotions, rhythms, and melodies. Some people are so deeply rooted in one side of their brain that some activities involving the opposite hemisphere can be difficult for them—not impossible, but not exactly comfortable, and it takes some training and practice to overcome that difficulty.

In 1979, Dr. Betty Edwards published a groundbreaking book on enhancing creativity and improving drawing skills called *Drawing on the Right Side of the Brain.* In it, she explores a variety of techniques and exercises that help stimulate and enhance the right brain. It's packed with some really impressive before and after photos of real work by people utilizing her suggestions. What does this have to do with Spare, and the chaos magicians who modeled sigil technique on his work? I think that he created the initial-letter technique as a way to help jump-start left-brain thinkers. Crafting a statement and then removing all of the vowels and extra consonants from it forces you to look at those letters as shapes. It tasks you with the challenge of making it into an image in a MacGyver moment. To make an image, you need to tap into the right hemisphere and access the most intuitive part of your brain, which is key for magick. It's a tool to help you get used to thinking about images as having meaning, versus always thinking in words.

But if you're already adept at using your right brain, especially for art and magick, then that method is not going to feel very intuitive. It asks you to make a meaningful statement, strip it of meaning, and then reassign meaning to it. It's very back and forth. However, if you associate words with images, and those images can be merged together to create your sigil, you're making a straightforward procession from left to right brain. This steady progression from analytical thought to intuitive imagery is what sigil witchery is all about. It feels much more immediate and dynamic.

It's like the difference between performing choreography while thinking about it step by step versus actually dancing with the music and feeling the movements. Learning how to do the steps is integral to the process, but you need to be able to connect those steps with feeling and an overarching meaning to give the dance life. And sometimes you need to throw away the choreography and just move to the music.

With all that said, there's one very important thing to keep in mind: Everyone grasps information a little differently. There is no wrong approach. They all get you to the same place—just like walking, riding a bicycle, driving a car, or hopping on a plane can all get you where you need to go. All are forms of transportation, but some may be more efficient or better for time, distance, budget, health, or the environment. Still, they're all choices in the end. The sigil method that works best and is successful for *you* will be the right one.

CHAPTER 4
DESIGN GUIDANCE

Now that we've covered marks, shapes, and symbols, and gone in depth about the whys and hows of sigil witchery, we're going to get inside the designer's studio (aka the Witch's cottage). I'm going to share with you what I do to make sigils from a technical standpoint. I'll also provide tips and tricks to make the process smoother for you to learn and be confident in. We'll also explore the fabulous world of art supplies so you have a better understanding of what materials you can choose to work with.

SETTING UP FOR SIGIL WITCHERY

There isn't a lot of fuss that happens when I sit down to draw sigils, when creating for myself or anyone else. What's most important for me is having enough paper to draw on, a reliable pen, and a comfortable place to work. Once I get down to drawing, the rest of the world disappears. But I've also been drawing for most of my life—a kind of trance state comes naturally to me as soon as the pen touches the surface of the paper.

If drawing isn't your forte (yet!), then it may behoove you to take some time to prepare a clean and clear space for you to draw in. Make the environment comfortable for you (lighting, sound, chair, table, hot tea, cat), gather your drawing supplies, and sit down. Close your eyes and take three breaths, each one a little deeper and longer than the last one. Then open your sketchbook, grab something to draw with, and mark your paper with the date. (You can also add the time and location if you wish—it's really nice to have this information when you look back later.) Then consider the sigil you're going to make, going through the steps we talked about in the previous chapter. If the sigil is for someone else, put their name next to it, and begin to make your list of words. Consider the marks, shapes, and symbols those words represent, and build your sigil. Work at it until you get a design you are happy with. Over time, as you work more with sigils and drawing magick, your mind and body will recognize what you're intending to do, and naturally enter that light-trance focused state.

An Instant Sacred Sphere

Maybe you feel the need to create sacred space around you while you work, but you don't want to go into the process of ritually casting a circle or similar device. The idea behind circle casting is to create a container that protects in two ways: keeping whatever is happening inside the space *inside*, and preventing outside influences from disturbing the work. Although you may call upon the four cardinal directions in combination with the elements, it is indeed a sphere you are building, not a flat square. If you travel far enough in any direction, you will essentially end up coming from its opposite. Also, while elements may be associated with certain directions in a ritual sense, they are concepts that exist in all directions. I've already emphasized to you the power of your mind to create, so here is a very simple construct you can use to create immediate protective space around you:

From the east and to the west, an arching oval without rest.
From the north and to the south, close around me and all about.
From above and so below, follow with me wherev'r I go.

Simply think or say these words and visualize the structure of an atom surrounding you—you are the nucleus, and the directions and elements surround you like orbiting electrons. If you feel the need to the dispel the space cognitively as well, you can do that easily. Simply take a deep breath in, then exhale and push outward, releasing the orbits like how the sun breaks through clouds.

A Sacred Sphere of Energy

Note: If you start doing sigil work on a train or other mode of transportation that requires you to pay attention to outside stimuli, it's not my fault if you miss your stop. Hazards of the trade.

GETTING OVER GETTING IT WRONG

It's important not to get precious with your sigil exploration time. When I sit down with my blank page, my list of key words, or the name of the person I'm working on, I allow myself to be imperfect. I explore combinations and shapes, seeing what works and what doesn't. If I find that part of a sigil is working, I draw it again, and add in other elements until it feels balanced and complete to me.

Don't erase or scratch out anything! If you constantly erase every mark or cross out your work as you go along, you can't evaluate and compare. It's important to try out different compositions, angles, positions, and variations—and see instantly what works and what doesn't work when you pull back from the page. In the sketching stage of making a sigil, don't be nitpicky. Explore, and try out different combinations and orientations. If you do this, you will have a stronger sense of when your sigil ready. Constantly erasing breaks down your confidence and prevents you from seeing your progress. Sometimes a design you initially rejected has some elements you do want to use.

There is no shame in trying out ideas. Sometimes you'll arrive at the perfect design on the first try, and other times you may fill an entire page (or three!) before you find a sigil that works for you. There's nothing wrong with that. It's simply part of the design process.

Simple versus Complex

The general idea with sigils is to make them a simplified visual manifestation of your working. It helps to make them streamlined and reliably reproducible as necessary. Be careful about making your sigils too complex or "kitchen-sinking" them. Too many elements weigh down the design and complicate the message. Cleaner tends to be more direct and effective. Put enough marks in so you feel that the intention comes across clearly and feels complete without over-embellishing it. As you're designing, think about what elements can be combined. Do you need to have both an arrow and a star, or can they be combined into a shooting star? Can that horizontal line double as the top of an anchor or a bar of a scale?

There are situations where you can definitely indulge in making your sigil more ornate and complex, if you feel it works for the design. Getting elaborate with a sigil that will be reproduced only once—whether for a temporary usage or because the application of it will take only one time—makes perfect sense. Examples of this would be a painting for your altar or a tattoo—and the complexity may add to the overall energy and feel of the sigil in a way that feels right to you.

Avoid Pictures and Pantomime

On a similar note regarding simple versus complex drawings, keep in mind that you are not illustrating a scene here. Remember that symbols stand in for something else with greater meaning, so don't feel like you have to express every detail or be exceptionally literal in your sigils. Rather, it's best to move away from being overly representational. A sigil is a complex idea filtered down into a very simple image.

For example, when I teach theatrical dance, I talk about using body language and quality of movement to relay expression instead of relying on blatant symbols to cue the audience in. If you are sad or in mourning, you can reflect that in how you move without needing a Styrofoam gravestone prop to be on the stage or dripping tears with crying-like gestures to express your grief. Props, spelling things out blatantly, representational pictures—all of these can overcomplicate the message. This approach doesn't allow for as much imagination or drawing new connections on behalf of the viewer.

The same is true for sigils: you're not telling a story like in a book or play, outlining every scene—you're crafting a succinct spell. The sigil is more than the sum of its parts; it's the progression of those ideas merging into a new idea. Don't get hung up on the parts to find meaning. Allow it to take on its own form.

I would like to note here, though, that fully representational works of art *can indeed* be used for magick. It's just a different approach and method than sigil witchery. I often create paintings for spellcraft that use recognizable subject matter represented in a realistic or surrealistic way, sometimes with sigil work incorporated into them. Creating that kind of artwork is very different from your left brain dictating that you must have complex symbols and a storyline to make your sigil. Visionary artwork is steeped in expressing inner vision and liminal experiences, based in the language-less theater of the right brain. The left brain often clings to complex, easily recognized symbols for logical reasons; it prefers to be safe and contained. You want to be able to push past those surface associations and go deeper when designing your sigils.

Why Draw Your Own Sigil?

This part is for the person who may be asking, "But can't I just copy someone else's sigil? That sounds easier!" I suppose you could *if* that sigil really resonates with you *and* you take the time to sit down and connect with it. Symbols generally gather meaning because people resonate with them. For example, the Power Sigil I created (see it in chapter 6) was specifically designed for anyone to use. I didn't sit down to create it for myself. My intent was to make a sigil that anyone who felt they needed power could connect with and use. As I drew it, I thought about all the different kinds of people who might find it useful in their lives, and what they were facing. Similarly, I draw sigils for clients who trust in my expertise to make something especially attuned to them. The sigil then belongs to them specifically, and they follow through with the application and acknowledgment.

But if you're thinking, "Oh, I'll just copy this sigil someone else made instead," because you don't want to take the time to craft your own, then you're probably *not* going to achieve the desired effect. Sigils are very personal—they are created with your own intent for yourself or while focused on the needs of someone else. A healing sigil that I create for Jessica's physical injury is not going to be like the healing sigil I create for Steve's emotional issue. Both involve healing, but they are different people with unique needs and problems. So don't be lazy.

Drawing Tech

There really is only one way to build up your drawing skills: PRACTICE! I so often hear the excuse "but I can't even draw a straight line with a ruler," yet all of us drew confidently as children. If you don't consider yourself much of a drawer, but you *can* write with a pen or pencil, it's time to ditch that baggage telling you that you can't draw. And those of you who have gotten hooked on coloring books know how meditative and relaxing it can be to put pen or pencil to paper. The same is true for freestyle drawing. It's often why we doodle when we're on the phone or bored. It occupies the mind without taxing it. Drawing shapes without having a guide to follow is not terribly difficult; it just takes some practice and a dash of confidence. Sigils do not have to be perfectly straight to work. You just need to understand the symbolism in the marks made.

Most importantly, give yourself the chance to improve. Don't look at your first drawings and think it's hopeless. Keep drawing, and build familiarity with holding that pen, pencil, or brush. It's no different than learning to use a new mouse, keyboard, or game controller—you just need to keep using it to become familiar with it. Pretty soon you will get the hang of it!

About Tracing

I'm all for tracing as a means of meditation (see the "Acknowledging Your Sigil" section in the previous chapter), going over the lines of a sigil again and again to achieve a trancelike state. But I don't believe tracing is more helpful in teaching you to draw than is freestyling it. Consider the relationship of tracing to drawing like the way training wheels work on a bike; you don't quite get the balancing trick of riding a bike until those wheels are really off and you're on your own. So while tracing can help you get more familiar with a shape, it's best to start seeing the shape in your mind's eye. Then from there you are pulling it forth through your hand to create new shapes and onward to sigils!

Drawing Instructional

I've included here some breakdowns of some of the more intimidating shapes to help you along. You can definitely use rulers, tracing tools (found in the graphic design departments of art and office supply stores), compasses, and protractors, but I suggest building your ability to draw freehand. It increases your eye-hand coordination skills and your confidence in your drawing abilities. Sure, things may look rough at the start, but that's what practice is all about.

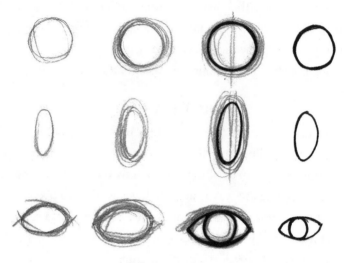

Drawing Circles and Ovals

Circles

I remember exactly where I was when I learned how to draw more perfect circles and ovals. I was six years old and in a formal drawing class, tasked with drawing a candlestick and holder. It has stuck with me all these years. Whether you're drawing a circle, oval, egg, or other kind of ellipse, allow yourself to sort out the shape by softly drawing overlapping spheres. Choose the one that's closest to the desired shape and outline it in pen. Erase the additional marks.

In each row of the illustration here, columns 1–3 show building up concentric circles and ovals to get a precise, clean shape, versus column 4, drawn without guidelines.

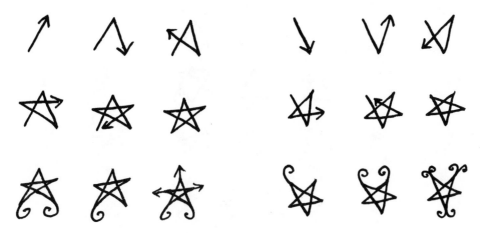

Drawing Pentagrams

Five-Pointed Stars (Upright, Inverted)

To create an upright pentagram, it's easiest to start in one of the bottom corners (left or right tends to depend on your dominant hand—I start in the bottom left) and draw upward. To draw an inverted star, start at a top corner, and go downward.

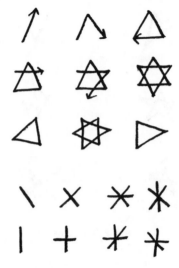

Drawing Six-Pointed Stars

Six-Pointed Stars

The easiest way to draw a traditional six-pointed star is by first drawing an upright equilateral triangle (all sides equal). Then on top of the first triangle, draw a triangle of equal size but pointing downward. If you'd like to draw more of an asterisk version of a six-pointed star, start by drawing an X. Then draw a horizontal line through the middle of the X. Or you could choose to draw a vertical line through the center instead. The key is to plan ahead so that when you make the six "slices," they're somewhat evenly spaced.

Drawing Seven-Pointed Stars

Seven-Pointed Stars

Seven-pointed stars take a little more planning, but they're not that much more difficult to draw than a five-pointed star. However, I do find it easier to work the lines in pairs so you don't lose your spot or forget where you're heading next. It also helps to see the base shapes as a *Star Trek* motif or Pontiac logo. Follow the illustration to see how to draw your own.

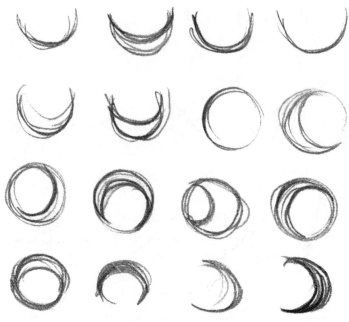

Drawing Crescents

Crescents

Similar to the circle method, draw overlapping U's until you get the shape you want for your crescent on the inside and outside. You can also sketch out circles to get your main outside line, and then decide how thin or wide you'd like your crescent to be inside of it. Ink the one that works for you and erase the rest of the extra lines.

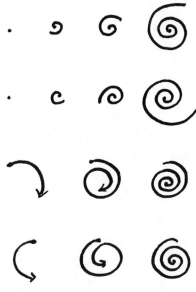

Drawing Spirals

Spirals

Spirals are easy to draw, right? They are! But have you thought about how you draw your spiral? I have included this shape here because I want you to consider two methods of drawing spirals. In one method you start at an internal point and slowly circle out from it, expanding out. The inverse is to start drawing a curve and continue drawing inside of it, smaller and smaller. These tend to not only look different but feel different as well when you draw them. The inside-out spiral feels expansive and open, seemingly reaching outward toward infinity. The outside-in spiral slowly constricts upon itself—it's contained and definite. Which spiral you draw depends on what your goal is with it.

OMG Art Supplies!

Going shopping for art supplies can be either an exciting or a daunting experience. There's so much to choose from that it can be overwhelming—or inspiring! I'll be your personal shopping buddy to help you make some excellent choices when it comes to buying art materials.

Everybody has a type of shop where they always feel like a kid in a giant candy store. For me, that place is anywhere that sells a decent selection of art supplies. Of all the jobs I've worked over the years, one of my favorites has to be when I was in college and did work study at the Rhode Island School of Design art store. I was totally immersed in all kinds of art supplies—learning about them, stocking them, helping other people find them, making recommendations, getting free samples—and I got an employee discount on top of my student one!

Which reminds me: by the way, folks, art supplies are not cheap—at least not the good ones that will last a long time and are easier for you to use. Dollar stores and big-box brands may seem like they are cheaper, but they are rarely archival, run out quickly, and may be full of harmful chemicals. Not that more expensive art supplies are automatically safer (cadmium, anyone?), but they pass more rigorous health standards and include proper labeling more than bargain supplies do. So do some research before buying your art supplies and you'll get something that will be less of a headache to work with and may last a lifetime.

Also, if you can go to a real art supply store, there's a really good chance that the people working there are also artists. Which means they tend to know a lot about what's available, what works, and what sucks, and they'll be happy to answer your questions. That is not usually the case at big-box office supply and craft stores, nor are their prices really that much better—though the occasional coupon can get you a good deal on a pricier item.

Sketchbooks

I recommend getting a small sketchbook to work in, preferably one that is marked "drawing" paper, as it's usually about 80 lb. paper (the calculated weight of a ream of paper), which makes for a nice medium thickness of paper. I like a bit of room to move around on a single sheet of paper without getting cramped, so my ideal size of book is usually 8 x 10 or 9 x 12—which is also the same size as my scanner bed. I also like square books, although there's no logical reason for why, besides the neat shape. There are all sorts of sketchbooks on the market, from true-bound to spiral-bound, hardcover to papercover ones. Be sure the one you choose is marked "archival," or it may start to yellow and fall apart on you rather quickly. That's also good advice if you're looking to make a book of shadows or a grimoire out of a sketchbook—you want it to last!

About Paper Type and Texture

The texture for "drawing" grade sketchbooks tends to be fairly smooth, with just enough "tooth" to it to make it easy to work on. Hot press paper—watercolor or Bristol—is extra smooth, which can be slippery to work on but makes for really smooth, clean lines. Cold press paper is extra rough, giving you that classic "watercolor" paper effect. It's really not ideal for drawing. Newsprint is good for figure drawing class, but it's not archival, and the paper tears very easily. It's meant for charcoal, not pens and pencils. It may look like a lot of paper for cheap, but don't be fooled—get the proper drawing tablet with the archival paper!

Graphite Pencils

H to the B! You may remember needing 2B pencils for taking standardized tests in grade school. Pencils have a range of graphite hardness to softness that's known as the HB scale, where H is light and B is dark/blackness. The letters are also paired with numbers. The higher the number, the farther it is on the scale toward its extreme. The higher the number paired with the H, the harder the lead and the lighter the mark. Similarly, with B, the lead is softer and makes a darker mark. So if you want to lightly sketch out your sigils before you ink over them, I'd recommend getting a 4H or 2H pencil, because they are very easy to erase and don't make too much of an indentation on the paper. Once you get into the B's, it will become increasingly harder to erase your marks. For just standard sketching with a pencil that provides a smooth and dark line, I'm a big fan of the 6B. You don't have to press hard to make a dark mark, which is very helpful to avoid cramping up your drawing hand! Similarly, there is the Ebony brand pencil that's essentially a 6B, usually a little less expensive than the marked pencils.

Tip: Invest in a good manual sharpener, preferably one that has a container attached to it to catch the shavings. Electric sharpeners eat up soft pencils like crazy.

Mechanical Pencils

The easiest mechanical pencils to find are the ones that you just push-click and that come a dozen or so to a bag. However, they have a small, sharp lead that can easily dig into your paper, plus they are prone to snapping and breaking. So yes, they're convenient for having a sharp point, but they're annoying for disrupting your line trance. There are fancier mechanical pencils out there that are designed for drafting (engineering and architectural plans). They can be really nice—with a price tag to match, but they are designed to be refillable. If this interests you, I'd recommend going to an art store and testing them out to see if you like them.

Erasers

Forget pink erasers. I don't know whose lame idea those were, but they can stain your paper and don't erase well. There are essentially three real erasers on the market to look for: white vinyl erasers, kneaded erasers, and gum erasers. Vinyl ones tend to clean up the best, kneaded ones don't produce any debris (and you can "knead" them clean, which is also great stress relief), and gum erasers (which often get confused with kneaded erasers, because the latter often look like gray gum and are pliable) work better for some mediums and surfaces.

Tip: Many art shops carry basic drawing kits (often for a reduced package price) that come with an assortment of pencils and erasers so you can try them out and see what you like.

Colored Pencils

If you're into coloring books, then you've probably already developed some preferences for colored pencils. Pretty much the only ones I bother with are the Prismacolor brand. They are definitely more pricey, but they have a smooth, consistent texture and fantastic color coverage. There are also water-soluble colored pencils and fancy crayons that you can draw with and then go over those marks with a wet brush, to get a mix of drawn and painted effect.

Pens (by Level)

Easy: One of my favorite tools for sketching is also one of the cheapest out there: your basic ball-point Bic pen. This kind of pen makes a fine line that can be even finer and lighter with a light touch and heavier/darker when you press down harder. You also can't erase your mistakes, so it can teach you to be more focused on how you are drawing, as well as allow you to build up a tableau of sketches instead of being tempted to erase and start over again and again. These types of pens are often available for cheap to free at your local bank, pharmacy, hotel, etc. (I mean the ones they give away. I'm not advocating stealing them.)

Medium: When I'm working on a final design to send to a client, I often draw the sigil using a Micron pen by Sakura. They come in a variety of colors and nib (tip) sizes and have archival ink. You can go from super fine (005) to fine (01) to medium (03, 05, 08) to thick (1, etc.). The 05 thickness is typically my go-to for line work. The super-fine tip is easy to damage, and the 01 tends to dry out faster. The 05 can take a beating, yet makes a nice viewable, clean line without bleeding or getting blocky. These pens cost between two and three dollars apiece.

Traditional Pen and Ink

Expert: You can always go old school (and technically more ecofriendly than the disposable pens just mentioned) by investing in a pen base, metal nib, and bottle of ink—or a feather quill if you're extra-adventurous. You can try out all sorts of interchangeable nibs for your pen base, from drawing ones to calligraphy tips. This kind of pen is definitely a tool that takes a fair bit of practice to use, and even then, a fiber in the paper can catch the nib and cause a blob of ink to collect. I tend to hold all of my pens fairly close to the base, so I often end up with inked hands as well, despite my best efforts. If I want something more organic, I replace the pen and nib with a fine paintbrush, as I feel I have more control over how the ink runs through the bristles. (See the upcoming section on brushes.)

Gel Pens

Gel pens come in an insane number of colors, including pearly, metallic, and sparkly finishes. They often provide a smooth drawing experience. They are especially handy for drawing on dark surfaces (like black paper). However, they can be pricey, and some brands don't last very long, so invest in a couple of colors you want before buying a big set (usually filled with nearly identical colors you won't ever use).

Sharpies and Other Permanent Markers

Sharpies are the king of permanent markers! Need to write on metal, glass, or plastic? Black Sharpies will do it. They also make very nice gold and silver metallic Sharpies, which I prefer over the fancier metallic pens that require you to shake them constantly and push on the tips, all the while smelling really bad. A note about odors: While Sharpies don't smell quite as bad as other permanent markers, I don't recommend using them for tiny details or in an enclosed space with your nose practically on top of the marker. Use Microns instead, because they are odorless and achieve better details without making you sick.

Tip: You can clean up or remove the marks made by most brands of permanent markers on non-permeable surfaces with rubbing alcohol. Try a small area first with a cotton swab lightly dipped in the rubbing alcohol to make sure you won't damage the surface.

Dry Erase Markers

Need to mark a non-porous surface for a very temporary amount of time? Dry erase markers may be your buddies, but they don't always work on all things, so test your surface first. They are especially handy for drawing on mirrors and other kinds of glass surfaces.

Brushes

If you haven't looked at a brush since you used a camel hair one in grade school with poster paints, you may be in for a bit of a shock. Remember Ollivander's Wand Shop from Harry Potter? It's kind of like that. No, the one true brush for you isn't made of unicorn hair—but when you look at the price, you might think it was!

Kinds of Brush Tips

   Good brushes are a big investment for artists—and there are hundreds to choose from, varying in shape, size, and material. For starters, I recommend looking for a brush with synthetic hairs that feel smooth and silky to the touch. I prefer the round and rounded tip varieties, especially the Winsor & Newton University Series 233 brushes. The smaller the size (000, 00, 1, 2), the smaller the tip; the larger the size (3, 5, 8, 12, 14), the larger the tip. Look at how the bristles are arranged—each gives you a different kind of line quality. Round, pointed round, and detail tip shapes are especially good for creating fine, consistent lines. Flat and bright shapes are better for making bigger, bolder strokes and covering larger surfaces. A filbert shape is good for blending. An angular flat or chisel shape will give a sort of calligraphy effect to your strokes, as you can work the brush to get both thinner controlled marks and wide bolder ones.

Consider the scale of your project when selecting brushes. If you're working on a large format (like a mural), then you'll want bigger brushes. If you're working on something very small and refined, then you'll want to choose a much smaller brush. If you're overwhelmed and unsure, look for a starter kit or sample pack. They usually include half a dozen differently shaped and sized brushes.

Ink, Pigment, and Paint

If you thought the brush aisle was overwhelming, prepare yourself for the paint aisles! So many kinds of paint, so many colors, so many tubes and jars! Really, all you need is a jar of archival India ink (the one I currently have has a nice little squeezy dropper on top, which makes it easy to dispense some ink into a ceramic dish and add water to it as needed) or whatever color pleases you. But in case you're wondering what all of these paint types are, here's a quick and dirty list:

Oil Paint: pigment suspended in linseed oil; requires turpentine for cleaning; takes a long time to dry (permanent finish)

Acrylic: pigment suspended in acrylic resin; uses water for cleaning; dries quickly (permanent finish)

Watercolor: transparent pigment suspended in gum arabic; uses water for cleaning; dries quickly (not permanent)

Gouache: opaque pigment suspended in gum arabic; uses water for cleaning; dries quickly (not permanent)

Tempera: dry pigment mixed with egg yolk and water per use; uses water for cleaning (permanent finish)

Paint Grades: Every paint has a grade, usually marked from student to professional. Student grade colors tend to be less true in tone and synthetically produced, with the binding element being of average quality. Professional grade paints are usually made of pure pigments and the best binders.

CHAPTER 5
PRACTICE EXERCISES

In this chapter I'm going to walk you through some imaginary scenarios to demonstrate how I may go about creating a sigil for each, if presented with that situation. I've also included ideas for sigil application and acknowledgment where possible. *Note:* All scenarios here are completely fictional but are modeled on common occurrences that you might find familiar.

Before you start reading, pull out a pen and paper so you can do it yourself, too. I've set this up so that you can read about the scenario on one page, make your own notes and sketches, then flip to the solutions afterward to see what I've done. There is no wrong way—what you draw may look completely different. It's the process of thinking about it and trying it out for yourself that is the most important. Now let's make some happy little sigils!

SCENARIOS

Scenario: A Festival Sigil

It's the first day of the weeklong festival Pword Power Gathering! [13] As part of the opening ceremony, the attendees have gathered to create a sigil for this year's festival. The producers have put a call out for words that embody what everyone would like to experience at this year's festival. Since

---

13. *Pword* is my catch-all term for Pagans, Polythiests, Pantheists, etc.

it's a seven-day event as well as their seventh annual event, they've decided to pick seven words from the submissions. The selected words are *unity, love, understanding, inspiration, safety, energy,* and *happiness.*

Scenario: A Coven Sigil

The New Crescent is a newly formed coven, off-shooting from the Full Moon Coven and Tradition of Witchcraft—with permission. It is made up primarily of second-generation Witches who are children of members from the initial coven, all now in their late teens to early twenties—and some new folks who are of a similar age. They want to create a sigil to identify and represent their group. Their name, the New Crescent, refers back to the Tradition while signifying they are a new cycle. There are currently six members, and each one has chosen a word or phrase to represent what they wish to get out of working in the coven. Those words are *foundation, finding identity, wisdom, growth, mastering skills,* and *balance.*

Scenario: A Business Plan Sigil

Michael is starting a new business. Technically it's a developing side business for him, as he already has a tech job that he enjoys, but his weekend and evening experiments of crafting incense have been really successful at small events. He loves doing it and would like to grow the business more, but he isn't ready or prepared to give up his tech job. He's looking for steady growth, and he wants to do only limited batches so he's not producing the same thing over and over. The name he's using for his business is "Censered Scents." He's creating a web presence for his business and has done the legal paperwork so he can sell at shows and other events. His plan involves making one special incense every month, offering monthly subscriptions as well as the ability to buy directly through the website as long as supplies last. He wants a sigil that is both a logo and a business plan to put on all of his packaging.

Scenario: An Office Ward Sigil

Pearl works in a cubicle, like most of the people in her company. Certain coworkers seem to stop by a little too often for non-business chat, and that behavior is disrupting her work. She doesn't actively engage them or encourage them to hang out and chat; they're the floor gossips and busybodies. She's tried to be nice and to be direct, but it doesn't seem to be helping. It's a conservative company in a similarly conservative area, so Pearl wants to create a hidden sigil to put up that will make them leave her alone and won't be obvious or raise questions.

Scenario: A Healing Sigil

Geraldine, age forty, has been battling breast cancer. She has had a double mastectomy and undergone radiation. She is in remission and the prognosis looks good. She has decided against having reconstructive surgery and is adjusting to the new shape of her body. Geraldine wants a sigil that she will get tattooed on her chest. It will signify the battle she's undergone, give her strength and vitality, help her heal both physically and emotionally from her experience, and aid her in rediscovering herself and reclaiming her sensuality and sexuality.

Scenario: A Transformational Sigil

Marissa was born with the name of Marcos and the gender assignment to match, but she never felt at home in her body or being designated as male. At the age of twenty-nine, after much soul-searching, she decided to fully embrace her identity as a woman in all areas of her life. It has been a somewhat difficult experience with her family and for some of her friends, but they are slowly coming around. Marissa wants a sigil to continue to empower her as she undergoes physical changes, protect her from those who would harm her, and aid in helping her family understand and embrace the transition.

Scenario: A Sigil against Bullying

Christopher is twelve years old and a sixth grader. He is a good student, loves animals, and is a budding theater kid. Lately he's been targeted by fellow classmate Hank, who has been calling Christoper names, pulling pranks on him, and basically being a bullying jerk. Despite Christopher reporting Hank's behavior to teachers, which resulted in detention and a parent-teacher conference, Hank is still bothering him and his friends. Christopher asked his mom to sign him up for self-defense classes so he can better defend himself and others. You are good friends with his mom and know that Christopher is empathetic. As an extra measure, you decide to create a sigil that will build Christopher's confidence, as well as shield and protect him from bullying.

Scenario: An Anti-Anxiety Sigil

Danielle is a competitive swimmer who was diagnosed with general anxiety disorder when she was twenty-three. She takes medication to help her, and recently also began doing meditation and yoga. It's been a difficult path, but she feels like she's been slowly gaining control over her anxiety. Occasionally, though, she will have anxiety attacks when she's trying to fall asleep at night, and sometimes it manifests as insomnia as well. Her sigil will be a focus of meditation and designed to keep anxiety at bay, help her fall asleep more easily, and get more restful sleep.

Scenario: A Fertility Sigil

Brenna and Nick have been married for ten years. Three years ago they decided it was time to start a family, but despite their best efforts they have not yet been successful. It turns out that Brenna has a condition that makes conception difficult, but it may be overcome with medical intervention. She has been undergoing fertility treatments for the last year, and they are very hopeful. They are both new to the Pagan path, and Brenna has been personally drawn to the Greek goddess Demeter. She would like to craft a sigil that honors Demeter and will help her conceive a healthy baby, carry it to full term, and have a successful birth.

Scenario: A Focus Sigil

Vernon is going back to school to get a law degree at the age of thirty-nine. He had to drop out of college back in his twenties to take care of his mother, who had developed cancer, and care for his baby sister. His mom passed away two years later, and he focused on work to support himself and his sister. His sister is now grown, and he's decided it's time to go back to school. He's balancing his job, a promising new relationship, and his schoolwork. He has just two more semesters to finish up, and he wants some help to keep his eyes on the goal and keep everything in balance—or at least prioritized.

Scenario: A Banishing and Binding Sigil

Meg was in a relationship for six years with Kim, until she had to end it and move out two months ago. Kim is an alcoholic, currently refuses to get treatment, and gets both physically and verbally abusive. Meg got a restraining order and has been working on removing Kim from her life. Meg wants to do some magical work to keep Kim away from her, stop Kim from finding her, and stop Kim from further hurting herself or others.

Scenario: An Inspiration and Creativity Sigil

Alex is a talented professional artist who suffers from clinical depression. Like many Aries, when he's making work, everything is great. But when the depression starts to kick in, he finds it difficult to work, essentially leading to a long slippery slope of inactivity and blockages. He gets into a cycle where he starts to worry that he won't have another creative idea again. Alex needs a sigil to help him overpower getting stuck in that sludge, and direct him to find inspiration and creativity when he's in doubt.

Scenario: A Prosperity Sigil

Liza has been working her butt off, but barely makes ends meet every month once all of the bills have been paid. She is very responsible with her budget and her activities, and works hard at promoting herself. If she could pull in three hundred dollars more a month for the next six months, Liza would feel that she could finally make some headway in clearing out her student loan and other debt and start saving money. She would like to be able to take a trip overseas within the next year to study with a mentor and expand her craft. It's time to manifest!

SOLUTIONS

Solution: A Festival Sigil

We have a community event with a spiritual root—and the triple correlation of the number seven (seven days, seven years, seven words). Our chosen words are *unity, love, understanding, inspiration, safety, energy,* and *happiness.* Let's consider what shapes and symbols align with each of these words:

unity—a circle or lines converging into one

love—a heart

understanding—When I consider this word, I think about communication, especially listening. A pair of mirrored crescents or chevrons might reflect this nicely.

inspiration—asterisks (sparks of creativity)

safety—could be a circle for protection, a shield, or a triangle (caution, slow down, pay attention)

energy—spirals

happiness—a crescent in a bowl position

A Festival Sigil

So we have some possible overlaps where a symbol or shape can embody more than one of our words, and we have the opportunity to repeat a motif at least seven times, or perhaps use the number itself. I decided to start with a circle (unity). Then I drew a spiraled heart (love) that both surrounds the circle and layers on top of it. I extended spiral tails at the bottom of the heart for energy. I noticed that a triangle was created naturally by the space between the bottom of the heart and the inner circle. The circle felt empty to me, so I mirrored another triangle on top of it (safety). For Inspiration and the number seven, I placed three asterisks below the heart, two above, and one on either side. I then finished the design with a pair of above/below crescents (happiness and understanding). The overall shape now reminds me of a body or being, which seems to be a great sigil shape for a community event.

For indoor events, I've drawn sigils on large pieces of paper that are then hung in a public place—near operations, registration, etc. For an outdoor event, though, paper won't last very long. The sigil could be drawn on paper, but the organizers should then prepare a piece of fabric to paint the sigil on to make a banner, or have a piece of wood suitable for painting. If the sigil is designed ahead of time, it could be included in the event program, made into stickers or temporary tattoos, screened on shirts, and so on. For on-site application, the design could be shared with body painters and henna artists for them to apply (as part of a ritual or as a vendor), or it could be copied onto smaller pieces of fabric and hung like mini-flags throughout the camp area as part of the opening ritual.

A Coven Sigil

Solution: A Coven Sigil

In this situation we have a sigil that will be a mark of identification for a coven. First, let's consider their name: New Crescent. What is a new crescent? It is the emerging sliver of a waxing moon, so we should be sure to incorporate a waxing crescent into this design. In addition, we have six ideas to consider: *foundation, finding identity, wisdom, growth, mastering skills,* and *balance*. Let's consider what shapes and symbols align with each of these words:

foundation—a horizontal line

finding identity—arrow, for direction

wisdom—perhaps a pyramid or an eye for insight

growth—roots, leaves, blossoms

mastering skills—star, inverted

balance—a scale

Again, since New Crescent is the name of the coven, and the sigil will be used not only for directing the energy of the coven for magical work but also as a symbol of the coven itself, I started my drawing with a waxing crescent moon. From there I played with an inverted star (mastering skills) within a pyramid (wisdom). I then saw the base of the pyramid as an opportunity to form the line for foundation as well as the base of the scale for balance. To form more of the scale, I added opposing crescent moons, as well as leaf-like shapes for growth. I felt a third leaf at the tip of the star/ pyramid balanced out the design. To connect the larger crescent moon to the star/pyramid/scale and add finding identity, I placed an upright arrow originating from the base of the star up through the large moon. The overall design reminds me of a weather vane, which suggests the ability to be able to change and shift direction as needed while maintaining balance. That is a very important trait in a working group.

The finished sigil could be made into a banner that can be hung up when the group meets, or perhaps an altar cloth for ritual. If the group has a website or other web presence, it could be an identifying mark for them online as well. They could invest in having necklaces made with the sigil on them—or make them themselves if they are so skilled.

A Business Plan Sigil

Solution: A Business Plan Sigil

The words I underlined here are *side business, grow, steady growth, limited batches, Censered Scents, logo,* and *business plan.* From the description, I understand that Michael wants to make this a successful side project with controlled growth that won't overwhelm him, which is essentially his business plan. The sigil will definitely be a logo, so he wants something that is simple yet recognizable. For logos, I especially like to consider the letters or initials that make up the name, which in this case is *C* and *S*. C is a crescent moon, and if we turn it on its back, it becomes a bowl or container. S is a wavy line, allowing for fluid motion—and it's also reminiscent of the shape smoke makes as it rises. By placing the S in the bowl of the C, I'm referencing a bowl of incense—that's controlled. I felt a triangle shape could either be used underneath the bowl for a point of balance (as pictured) or placed over the S to emphasize more controlled growth. On top, it reminds me of an incense censer that is swung on a chain (hence the play on words in the business name). As a designer, when presenting a client with logos, I prefer to give them a couple of choices. So I included a few variations for Michael to choose from.

Since this sigil was specifically designed to be a logo, Michael will be applying it to his business cards, website, product labels, etc., as part of his branding for Censered Scents. I would suggest a wine or deep purple background, with the lines in embossed or simulated gold tones.

An Office Ward Sigil

Solution: An Office Ward Sigil

In the description of this situation, it's not so easy to pick out or underline key words or phrases. We need to consider what Pearl's problems are, and what is the best way to solve them. She needs to redirect the attention of noisy/chatty coworkers away from her, making her invisible to them. But she will still need to be seen and acknowledged by those who will appreciate her productivity and respect her space. I decided to start with Pearl by symbolizing her as her namesake: a small open dot. For redirection, I made two arrows that intersect just above the open dot and point away from it. I gave each of the arrows spiraling tails, so that they contain their own energies within them. The arrows intersect in two places, forming a mandorla. In the center of that, I placed another smaller open dot, making it into an eye. The eye can symbolize the positive attention Pearl does want from the right people. The mandorla/eye with the two spirals above it also mimics a bee or insect shape. We can interpret that both as the busybodies being buzzed off as well as the hardworking, focused nature of the bee. I decided to place an asterisk above the spirals to balance out the large open dot and to symbolize new energy and possibilities.

Since Pearl wants this sigil to be hidden, and the majority of issues tend to happen while she's in her cubicle, she can hide the sigil somewhere near the entry of her space. Two good options would be to draw it on tape on the back of her name bar or on the flat area of the thumbtack that holds up her calendar. She could also draw it on the black plastic area on the back of her desk chair.

A Healing Sigil

Solution: A Healing Sigil

This sigil request has a lot of layers to it. We have a mature woman who has (for now) overcome breast cancer. She requires both physical and emotional healing in a variety of ways. She needs protection against the cancer returning, and continued strength and vitality. She needs to become familiar and comfortable with the changes that have happened to her body, and see it has a badge of honor from a victorious battle. And under all of that strong exterior, she wants to be able to feel sensual and sexy again. We also know how she wants the sigil to be applied—as a tattoo—so the lines need to be clean and not too fine or close together.

I decided to start by creating a shield for Geraldine, drawing a large circle with a cross in the center of it. It also doubles as a target area—for keeping a keen eye on the disease, as well as internal focus. I felt inclined to draw a small empty circle on either side of the large circle—perhaps a reminder of the breasts she has lost to surgery, but also a dual symbol representing that sensuality comes from inside. I extended the vertical line up and down out of the circle. At the top end, I crowned it with an upright-pointing pentagram for protection and internal strength. At the bottom end, I placed a small closed heart for her emotional well-being to be rooted and solid. The heart grows out of a pair of mirrored spirals like a blossom. The sigil felt like it needed a little more energy, so I put in four dots—one for each decade of life. The overall effect of the sigil with the combined shapes seems to be a feminine form that is strong and prepared to fight.

A Transformational Sigil

Solution: A Transformational Sigil

For Marissa's sigil, I noted the words *embracing identity as a woman, undergoing physical changes, protection, understanding,* and *transition.* The first symbol that came to mind was a heart, so I drew a pair of hearts meeting tip to tip. I also thought about the triangles that make up the classic six-pointed star, and how that shape is a blend of energy. The separate triangles can be found within those connected hearts, but they also make an hourglass form, which is often considered to be feminine, while also referring to time and patience—important elements for someone transitioning, as well as building understanding. I decided to open up the top heart so that it becomes a cup-like image, with the triangle inside filling it, either for protection (not allowing anything to go too deep) or because the cup is full of positivity. For another layer of protection, I gave the figure a pair of arrow "arms" coming out of the neck of the hourglass, each with three small vertical marks centered on them. Within the bottom heart shape, I placed three more lines, which makes four sections—representing her interactions with the larger world, with friends, with family, and with her innermost self.

For application, I can see Marissa having this sigil made into a necklace or bracelet that she wears every day. It might also make a very nice small inner-wrist tattoo that she places on her dominant hand. She could also draw it on her mirror so she can see it when she gets ready in the morning and prepares for bed at night.

A Sigil against Bullying

Solution: A Sigil against Bullying

What I like about this situation is that Christopher is a very aware and present sixth grader. He's doing what he can physically to defend himself—and others! We're looking at adding a little more metaphysical energy to the mix to protect him emotionally and mentally. The words I underlined were *build confidence* and *shield and protect him from bullying*. My go-to base symbol for this was an upright-pointing pentagram for confidence and protection. For extra shielding and protection, I enclosed the star in a pentagon, and then drew one more pentagon around that one. From each of the star's points, I extended arrows with slightly curling heads. They poke, but the curls prevent the points from sticking in too deeply, so Christopher doesn't get too entrenched in the process. To give the image a sense of depth and pattern and amplify its energy, I drew four lines in the space between the two pentagons, separating each section into five areas.

To apply this sigil, I can see it being made into a patch—either embroidered or painted—that goes on Christopher's backpack. It could also be placed in his coat under the label, and drawn on the bottoms of his sneakers. It has a superhero feel to it (especially if it's drawn in blue, red, and yellow), so it won't stand out in those situations—it will just look like a neat design!

An Anti-Anxiety Sigil

Solution: An Anti-Anxiety Sigil

For Danielle's situation, the words I made note of were *focus of meditation, keep anxiety at bay, fall asleep more easily,* and *restful sleep.* I was also conscious of her connection to water as a competitive swimmer. I started by making an eye shape to symbolize sleep, but that symbolism felt like it overpowered the design. I then flattened the bottom of the eye shape into a horizontal line to allude to restful sleep. I extended the ends of the top curving line, dropping them down below the horizontal line slightly and curling in gently, like eyelashes. I placed a slender crescent moon on top of the main shape, facing upward like a bowl. Floating on top of that, I placed an asterisk enclosed in a circle—representing the anxiety being contained and separated from the restful state. Finally, in the empty area of the eye shape, I placed repeating ripples, like the surface of water. The overall sigil feels very calm and serene.

I think that making this sigil into a painting and placing it either behind Danielle's bed, directly across from it, or above it (like on a tapestry / canopy) would be a wonderful way for her to meditate upon the symbol before going to sleep. If she wants something more subtle, it could be drawn onto a headboard or worked into a pillowcase. Another idea would be making a small eye pillow and filling it with lavender, then stitching the fabric with the sigil.

A Fertility Sigil

Solution: A Fertility Sigil

The purpose of this sigil is twofold: It's part devotional, as it's meant to honor the goddess Demeter, goddess of grain, harvest, and fertility, and a strong mother figure. The other part refers to conceiving and bringing to term a healthy baby. These ideas bring two strong images to mind: a grain shape for Demeter and a growing seed shape for the baby. So I started with a nice plump mandorla for the seed shape, then sprouted a vertical line out of the top of it. To mimic grain, I arranged five chevrons on the vertical line. The line splits the five chevrons into ten leaves, which also represents the number of years Brenna and Nick have been married. They made the decision to start a family three years ago, so at the top end of the grain I placed three dots (third time's the charm). At the other end, I gave the seed some spirals for its roots. Between the roots, I drew a small starburst to act as the catalyst for setting the seed to grow. Lastly, I flanked the body of the seed with a pair of crescent moons facing out to represent protection as well as a cycle.

I can see Brenna and Nick placing this sigil on their altar as a focal point, and/or somewhere on their bed frame where they can both see it. If the timing works, it could be drawn outside in alfalfa sprouts (they germinate quickly) in fertile soil, and tended to. Brenna could also have it painted in henna on her belly.

A Focus Sigil

Solution: A Focus Sigil

Vernon has a lot on his plate. I noted that he's balancing work, a new relationship, and school. We can also probably assume he's pretty close to his sister, so family as well. He's very close to finishing school successfully but is obviously feeling the stress. The sigil needs to help him keep focused and balanced, and to make sure he takes care of himself as well in the process. I started this design with an even-armed cross. I decided it needed a stronger focal point, so I placed a circle around the intersection, emphasizing that cross-hair effect, as well as protective energy for his goal. At the end of the bottom arm, I drew a stable triangle to represent wisdom and a strong foundation. At the top of that same arm, I placed an upright-pointing star, for ascension and academic excellence. For the horizontal arm ends, I placed a pair of hearts, creating a sense of emotional balance. Beyond each of them, I placed a closed dot. This represents that those relationships will be there for him and help him toward his goal. Lastly, I made a visual X with four arrows pointed inward, flying toward the center. They help direct attention and energy to Vernon's goal.

Vernon has two main tools for his schoolwork: a thick notebook that he physically takes notes in, and his laptop, where he writes his papers—and he carries them both in a canvas messenger bag. He could draw the sigil on the cover of the notebook, tape it to the outside of the laptop, and draw it on his messenger bag. Another interesting thing about Vernon is that he's really into penny loafers, complete with putting a shiny penny on each shoe. They remind him of his grandfather, his mother's father, who was a major father figure in his life when he was little. So Vernon could take a fine Sharpie marker and draw the sigil on one side of each penny, then place them (sigil side down) back in his shoes. In a way, because of his association with the shoes, he'll be calling upon his relatives who have passed on for their guidance as well.

A Banishing and Binding Sigil

Solution: A Banishing and Binding Sigil

It's pretty clear that Meg has been doing as much as she can to get Kim out of her life physically. She is seeking metaphysical protection for herself but is also compassionate toward Kim, despite wanting her out of her life. She doesn't want to stop Kim by hurting her, but would rather see her get better—and not damage anyone else either. So there are several different kinds of layers here: separating Kim out of Meg's life and obscuring the way while also preventing harm from coming to Kim or anyone else. These could be separated out into several sigils (one for protection, one for banishing, one for binding, etc.), but if you think about it, getting Kim contained and focused on a path of self-awareness and treatment could take care of a lot of the issues. She's at the root of the issues, so I decided to focus on her.

I started by drawing an inverted pentagram to represent Kim, because in this scenario I'm visualizing her being turned upside down like the Hanged Man in the tarot. Next I contained her in a circle, and then drew a bounding box around the circle. In the center of each side of the square, I placed an outward-facing chevron. These create a repeating K around the box, and also stand in for listening ears or funnels of information. I lined up three dots in front of the mouth of each chevron—medicine to be taken, and 3 x 4 = 12 for the Hanged Man again, as well as a year's time of holding. I wanted her energy to mirror back gently at her as well, so I placed an inward-facing crescent at each of the corners.

Meg could use a saltwater or herb-infused solution to mark her home, vehicle, office, etc., with the sigil to ward off Kim. She could also take a photo of Kim, draw the sigil on the back of it, and choose to either set it on fire and scatter the ashes away from her. Or she could put Kim "on ice" by placing the photo with the sigil in a plastic bag with some water, sealing it up, and then tossing it in the back of the freezer.

An Inspiration and Creativity Sigil

Solution: An Inspiration and Creativity Sigil
When considering Alex's situation, what stands out to me is that he needs to break free from cycles, keep momentum going when he needs it, and be open to change. What often happens when we get stuck in cycles is that we get focused on seeing in only one direction. In order to be open to inspira-

tion and creativity (and not get caught going in circles), we need to acknowledge more directions. So for Alex's sigil, I started off with a stylized six-pointed star, making the triangles themselves arrowhead-like in shape—one shooting up and the other down. At the singular top/bottom points of the triangles, I placed double chevron "heads" accenting each direction. At the base points of each triangle, I placed double "tail" chevrons, to give an added sense of direction. Then I added spiral-like wings to either side of the star, which also forms a stylized version of the zodiac symbol for Aries while giving a sense of flight or lightness. Lastly I placed two asterisks at either end of the directional points, to signify inspiration and goals. The overall sigil gives a strong sense of movement, that either direction is the correct one, as long as you keep moving.

My suggestion for Alex to apply his sigil is to have it somewhere in his studio where he can see it—perhaps on a desk, easel, or doorway. If he's so inclined, he may consider getting it tattooed. Another thought, if Alex is into ritual processes, is that he could light some stick incense and "draw" the sigil with the smoke when he feels like he's hit a block. Or if he works on canvases, he could take a brush with just water on it and draw the sigil on the surface of a canvas before he gets down to work.

A Prosperity Sigil

Solution: A Prosperity Sigil

In this scenario, we have immediate needs/goals that in time will allow for bigger goals to be achieved. Liza has a very specific goal of bringing in another three hundred dollars a month for six months. In her profession, that amount of money could be made just by getting one or two more gigs each month. The sooner she starts, the faster she can get to planning a trip overseas that will boost her career. To start on this sigil, I considered math rooted in the number six: 6 x 50 = $300. We're also looking at a period of six months. And the Six of Swords in the tarot symbolizes travel, usually to new places. So to reflect this math, I made a horizontal line overlaid with an X. In the middle of each "sword" I made an outward-facing chevron for a "hilt." Then I tipped each of the swords with a five-petaled flower. These represent the potential for money opportunities to blossom. We can get the magnifying power of ten from the initial X. Finally I drew a large petal in between each intersecting line to focus the energy on the center of the whole sigil.

Liza may not have a lot of extra money right now, but she does have a large jar of dried thyme in her kitchen cabinet, and the moon is almost full. She can easily make a paste out of the thyme and some water, and squeeze it out of a plastic bag with a small hole cut into the tip. From there she can draw the sigil on the floor of the balcony of her apartment. For an added touch, she can place coins on the center of the sigil and each of the flowers.

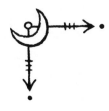

CHAPTER 6
GALLERY

I thought you might find it inspiring to look at a collection of sigils that I have made—for myself, for general use, and for clients. I've also included some artwork I have made that includes sigil work.

THE POWER SIGIL

It was the day after the 2016 US presidential election, and the mood around the house, our city, and the majority of our friends and family was rather grim. I don't do well being idle, nor feeling helpless. I needed to do *something* that would be productive, that would have meaning and impact. So I did what comes naturally to me: I made a sigil for others to use, and I posted it on my blogs.

The following text is what I prefaced the Power Sigil with:

So much is at stake, at risk, and in danger—yet these are the times we were made for. I seek to exchange my tears of fear and dread—for those of determination, spawn by the winds of revolution. I have put brush to paper, intent into action, by crafting a sigil for all of you who need protection and guidance against the impending storm. To summon its power and remind you of your own. To be a beacon to get us to the time of the Star, navigating safely through the time of the Tower.

Upright Power Sigil

Inverted Power Sigil

Description of the Power Sigil and the Meaning of Its Parts

The largest part of the form is a five-pointed star, representing protection and the elements that make us up: earth, air, fire, water, and spirit. Within that star is a second star, another layer of protection and a balance of conflicting identities, shining against the dark and the unknown. Within that star is an open circle representing an egg, a seed of truth, the eye of calm within, potential. Extending out from each arm of the larger star are tripled-barbed arrows. They guide our energy outward, reaching while protecting, their points digging deep into what they pierce. Flanking each internal chevron of the star is a crescent moon—its horns protecting the vulnerable areas while also representing the waxing and waning of the moon, of ideas, of waves. There is one moon for each of the next four years, with a fifth to mark the rising of a new era of hope and change. Behind each crescent is a black dot—a point of origin or destination, a new moon's energy of facing fears and banishing the dark within and without.

I present the Power Sigil to you here in two variations: upright/upward-pointing and inverted/downward-pointing. I believe that the star, regardless of its direction, represents duality, both masculine and feminine energies. The intent of the sigil is the same for either direction, but one may appeal more visually to you and/or be more safe for you to use in the face of ignorance. It is a mark to remind you of your own power, and to take action.

I welcome you to share this sigil, to use it in your home, at work, on your body. You can print it out to look at, draw it again and again for yourself, make into a talisman, tattoo it on your body, trace it during meditation—whatever helps you activate it. I ask that you simply please respect my copyright of the design by not reproducing it for profit, and contact me for permission for additional uses or questions.

Thank you and so mote it be.

#witchpower

Festival Sigils

The following are examples of festival sigils. At each event where I teach my workshop, the class collectively works together with me to craft a sigil for the occasion as part of the learning process. We talk about what we'd like to get out of the event throughout the course of it—and perhaps what we will come home with—for ourselves, for our paths, etc. We brainstorm a list of words, and then go through each word and consider how we'd like that word to be presented. It's a collaborative experience that's always a lot of fun. I've included a few of these sigils, along with their associated lists of words.

PantheaCon Sigil

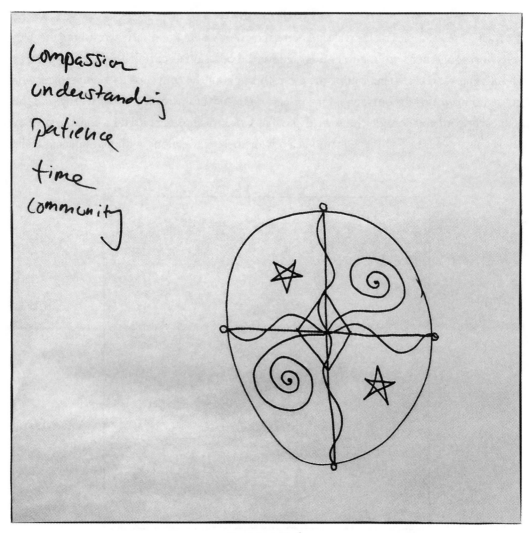

Compassion
understanding
patience
time
community

Paganicon Sigil

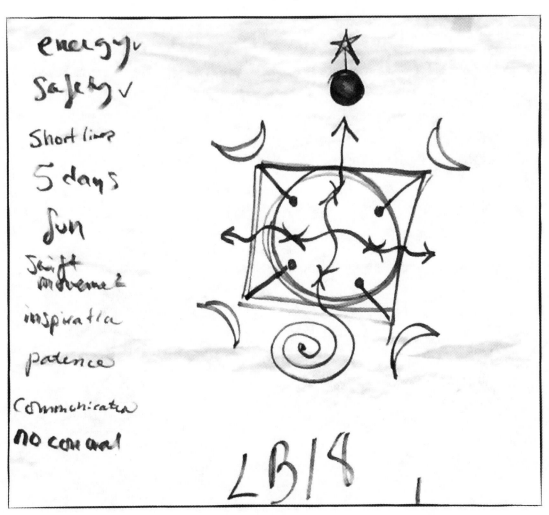

energy ✓
safety ✓
short time
5 days
fun
Swift
movement
inspiration
patience
communication
no control

DragonCon Sigil

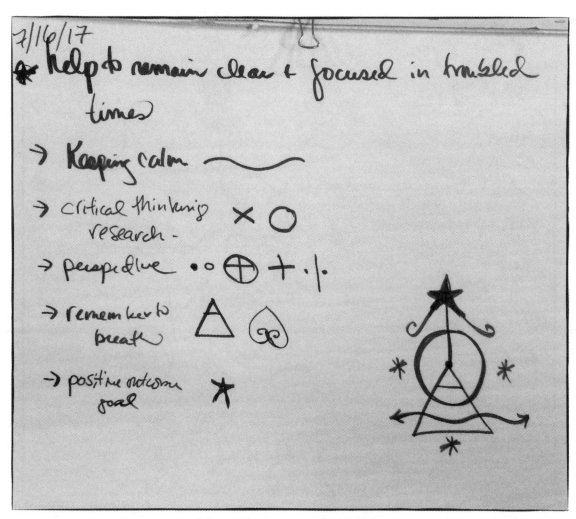

7/16/17

★ Help to remain clear + focused in troubled times

→ Keeping calm ~~~~

→ critical thinking research - ✕ ○

→ perspective •• ○ ⊕ + •|•

→ remember to breath △ ♡

→ positive outcome goal ★

Workshop Sigil at Herne's Hollow in Delaware

THE ARTIST'S SKETCHBOOK

I've noticed an interesting thing about how my notetaking has evolved since my days in academia. Back then I would make notes for homework, important points to remember for tests, detailing processes and procedures. Nowadays, if I'm taking notes I'm probably at a convention or conference of some sort. If I'm not up on the panel or presenting, then I'm sitting in the audience probably doing one of two things: writing down counter-ideas/thoughts to what is being said, or sketching while I absorb what I'm hearing. The former involves largely my left brain working in overdrive as I evaluate what I'm hearing and process counter-arguments or agreements in my head. The latter is almost like recording a record. It may seem like I'm doodling, but later when I look back at the image, I can remember a great deal of what was said. The image doesn't even have to have anything to do with what the topic was for me to remember it (although often it's inspired by it).

Similarly, when I'm working on paintings and listening to podcasts or the radio, I can often remember what story was being told at the time and how I felt about it, all by just looking at the painting—or a print of the painting! It doesn't work quite the same way with music playing in the background, though. Music tends to sit back, while things I'm thinking about in my head move to the forefront. This is why I prefer to listen to something with a story, like a podcast, when I'm making art. It cancels out the talking part of my own brain, leaving it out of the conscious equation of the art-making process.

Sigil Crafting and Notetaking

Another Sketchbook Page

Mago Djinn Sigil

Mago Djinn is the part of my business where I focus on design, sigil witchery, and modern folkwear designs—www.magodjinn.com. To craft this sigil, I took *M* and *D* as my starting points, and considered what I wanted to do with this concept and where I wanted it to take me.

Mago Djinn Sigil

Custom Sigils

As part of my Patreon account, I've been designing sigils for those participating at certain levels and above. They describe to me what they're looking for, and I create the sigil. Here are some samples.

Jaime's Sigil: grounding, creativity, fortune, inspiration, well-being, anxiety-free

This sigil has been included in memory of Jaime Johnson: 1980–2017. Jaime requested this sigil in the spring of 2017, and I provided a sketch for her then. Unfortunately Jaime tragically lost her life the following July, so I never got a chance to give her the digital version of her sigil. She was truly a beautiful and vibrant person, so I am choosing to include her full name, her request, and the finished sigil here to honor and remember her. Rest in power, Jaime <3

Jaime's Sigil

Carolyn's Sigil: regain health, happiness, adventure, spirituality

Carolyn's Sigil

Jennifer's Sigil: adventure, balance, find momentum and focus

Jennifer's Sigil

Kim's Sigil: being present, not dwelling on the past or fretting about the future, labyrinth

Kim's Sigil

M's Sigil: positive thinking, protection, love, exploration, the Morrigan, Anubis

M's Sigil

Mary's Sigil: health and focus

Mary's Sigil

Matthew's Sigil: luck and prosperity

Matthew's Sigil

Megan's Sigil: restful sleep

Megan's Sigil

Paul's Sigil: finding happiness

Paul's Sigil

Stephanie's Sigil: doors opening, growth, creativity, spiritual path

Stephanie's Sigil

Veronica's Sigil: discipline, focus, harnessing energy and wisdom, heading into uncharted territory

Veronica's Sigil

THE MOTHER MATRIX

One of my most popular works of art to date is the *Mother Matrix*. What I think is particularly re-markable is that for the amount of meaning that many people see in her—and how much she has inspired people—she essentially came out of nowhere. A lot of my art is based on a specific idea or vision, then it comes into being. But there was no grand plan for the start of this piece.

Rather, a friend had talked me into vending at an event, mainly to keep her company. I didn't feel very comfortable at the event, and there were long stretches of time when it was really slow in the vending room. I set myself up with a drawing station, nearly hidden behind my display, and opened up a large sketchpad. I took a pencil and began mixing organic and geometric shapes into the form of a goddess-like figure. After a couple hours, the figure was complete, in pencil. I shared some work-in-progress shots online and was knocked over by the response. The next day I inked her (without screwing her up!).

The following weekend I was selected to do an Art in Action demonstration at Norwescon. I had recently picked up a couple of 1' x 2' birch panels, so I decided that I would translate the drawing into a painting for the demo. I prepared one panel with gesso and, while at the con, used India ink and water to outline the figure and do layers of washes over the course of the demo. After the con, I took her home, and within one to two days the whole painting was complete.

Since then, both the original drawing and the painting have found their way into prints, clothing, tattoos, and more.

The Drawing of the Mother Matrix

The Painting of the Mother Matrix

Other Artwork

As mentioned in chapter 3, I often incorporate sigil witchery into my paintings. I've included a few of them on the next few pages to show you what that looks like. Many of these pieces were originally done in full color—and you can see them in full technicolor online at www.owlkeyme.com.

The Iconomage series is an exploration of deities and Witch myths, all painted on reclaimed cedar panels that measure 3' tall x 5½" wide. Twenty pieces from this group I make available as full-size and ⅓-size giclee prints that I mount on wood and then hand-embellish. I call the full-size pieces "Temple" prints and the ⅓-size "Shrine" prints, as they allow collectors to create personal and immediate sacred space.

Familiar Territory is a mixed media painting on birch panel that measures 2' x 2' and was part of my "Witch Heart" solo exhibition in 2016. It explores elemental energies with animal/familiar spirits. (The original is in a private collection. Small prints are available.)

Queen of the Sabbat is a mixed media painting on reclaimed canvas that measures 32" x 40". This is the painting that inspired me to craft the sigils for my own legs. (The original painting is currently in the collection of the artist. Small prints are available.)

The Shaman is a mixed media painting on reclaimed canvas that measures 32" x 40". This motif is something I have been revisiting since the nineties when I first came across drawings based on "The Sorcerer," an image found at the Cave of the Trois-Frères in Ariège, France, made around 13,000 BCE. (The original painting is currently in the collection of the artist. Small prints are available.)

Details from Paintings from the Iconomage Series:
The Star Goddess • *The Huntress* • *Hekate* • *When Love Lay with Death and Darkness, Light Was Born*

Familiar Territory

Queen of the Sabbat

The Shaman

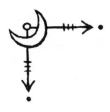

CONCLUSION

We have reached the end of our sojourn together into sigil witchery. I hope that you have found it illuminating and are inspired to try it out for yourself. Remember that it is perfectly valid to craft your own system of symbolism imbued with personal meaning. Your sigils don't have to look like my sigils or anyone else's, because they are yours. Don't be afraid to experiment, try out new techniques, and most importantly give yourself time to practice and build up your abilities. Also, don't be surprised if you start seeing the world around you with a new sense of insight. That tends to happen when you challenge yourself to see and think differently. Blessings and happy sigil making!

RESOURCES

ART AND SIGIL SUPPLIES

Alchemy Works: special inks, seeds for Witch herbs, and much more—www.alchemy-works.com

Blick Art Materials: Don't have an art supply shop near you? Check out www.dickblick.com

'Kəvən Craft Rituals: ritual ink, grimoires, and more—www.kevencraftrituals.com

Rosarium Blends: sigil ink and paper, among other lovely things—www.rosariumblends.com

Bibliography and Suggestions for Further Research

Art, History, and Culture

If you'd like to find out more about some of the artwork and cultures I have mentioned, here is a list to get you started. When it comes to art history and anthropology in general, try to find the most current versions of textbooks, as new information and research is always being uncovered.

Courtney-Clarke, Margaret (photographer). *Imazighen: The Vanishing Traditions of Berber Women*. Essays by Geraldine Brooks. New York: Clarkson Potter Publishers, 1996.

Critchlow, Keith. *Islamic Patterns: An Analytical and Cosmological Approach*. Rochester, VT: Inner Traditions, 1999.

Edwards, Betty. *The New Drawing on the Right Side of the Brain*. 1979. Reprint, New York: Jeremy P. Tarcher/Putnam, 1999.

Lewis-Williams, David. *The Mind in the Cave: Consciousness and the Origins of Art*. London: Thames & Hudson, 2002.

Lewis-Williams, David, and Thomas Dowson. *Images of Power: Understanding Bushman Rock Art*. Johannesburg: Southern Book Publishers, 1989.

Morphy, Howard. *Aboriginal Art*. London: Phaidon, 2007.

Stokstad, Marilyn. *Art History, Volumes I and II*. New York: Prentice Hall, 1995.

Von Petzinger, Genevieve. *The First Signs: Unlocking the Mysteries of the World's Oldest Symbols*. New York: Atria Books, 2016.

General Symbols and Magic

To check out the *Key of Solomon* and other esoteric works in the public domain, head over to www. esotericarchives.com.

Bruce-Mitford, Miranda. *The Illustrated Book of Signs & Symbols*. New York: DK Publishing, 1996.

Lunde, Paul, ed. *The Book of Codes: Understanding the World of Hidden Messages*. Berkeley, CA: University of California Press, 2009.

Paine, Sheila. *Amulets: Sacred Charms of Power and Protection*. Rochester, VT: Inner Traditions, 2004.

Parker, Derek and Julia. *The Power of Magic: Secrets and Mysteries Ancient and Modern*. London: Mitchell Beazley, 1992.

Pennick, Nigel. *The Book of Primal Signs: The High Magic of Symbols*. Rochester, VT: Destiny Books, 2007.

Pepper, Elizabeth. *Magic Charms from A to Z*. Newport, RI: The Witches' Almanac, Ltd., 1999

Ronnberg, Ami, and Kathleen Martin, eds. *The Book of Symbols: Reflections on Archetypal Images*. London: Taschen, 2010.

Austin Osman Spare

Interested in reading more about AOS and his influence on chaos magic? (A glass of whiskey is recommended as well.) Many of the books on AOS and his work are hard to find and/or rather pricey, but a good Google search will also get you excerpts of texts and PDF resources.

Baker, Phil. *Austin Osman Spare: The Occult Life of London's Legendary Artist*. Berkeley, CA: North Atlantic Books, 2014.

Carroll, Peter J. *Liber Null & Psychonaut: An Introduction to Chaos Magic*. York Beach, ME: Weiser Books, 1987.

Grant, Kenneth. *Images and Oracles of Austin Osman Spare*. Edmonds, WA: Holmes Publishing Group, 2003.

Spare, Austin Osman. *The Book of Pleasure (Self-Love)*. 1913. Reprint, Calgary, AB: Theophania Publishing, 2015. Also available in PDF format online.

GOOD STARTING PLACES TO EXPLORE OTHER SYMBOL SYSTEMS

There are many, many symbol systems out there. I've selected a few really good books in case you'd like to investigate some of the ones not covered in this book. These are ones that all have a home in my personal library.

Dominguez, Ivo, Jr. *Practical Astrology for Witches and Pagans*. San Francisco, CA: Weiser Books, 2016.

Flowers, Stephen E. *Icelandic Magic: Practical Secrets of the Northern Grimoires*. Rochester, VT: Inner Traditions, 2016.

Gray, Eden. *A Complete Guide to the Tarot*. New York: Crown Publishers, 1971.

Laurie, Erynn Rowan. *Ogam: Weaving Word Wisdom*. Stafford, UK: Megalithica Books, 2007.

Paxson, Diana L. *Taking Up the Runes: A Complete Guide to Using Runes in Spells, Rituals, Divination, and Magic*. Boston, MA: Weiser Books, 2005.

MAGICAL HERBALISM

Paul Beyerl's books are full of herb lore, history, uses, and magical associations—it's definitely worthwhile to have at least one of them in your library. Scott Cunningham's book is also an easy-to-use guide that tends to be readily available. Harold Roth's book focuses on thirteen specific herbs for

Witchcraft, but what is especially wonderful about it is that he focuses a lot on the growing aspects and working with the plants versus just lore, use, and history.

Beyerl, Paul. *A Compendium of Herbal Magick*. Custer, WA: Phoenix Publishing, 1998.

————. *The Master Book of Herbalism*. Custer, WA: Phoenix Publishing, 1984.

Cunningham, Scott. *Cunningham's Encyclopedia of Magical Herbs*. St. Paul, MN: Llewellyn, 1999.

Roth, Harold. *The Witching Herbs*. Newburyport, MA: Weiser Books, 2017.

WITCHCRAFT AND PAGANISM

There are many, many books on Witchcraft and Paganism out there, so here are a few of my favorites that I always recommend.

Drawing Down the Moon by Margot Adler: If you're interested in learning more about modern Paganism, this is the number-one book I recommend for getting an overall look at the history of Neo-Paganism and many of the branches you will find. Alas, Margot passed away in 2014, so we won't get any further updates from her, but I hope someone will carry the torch and keep track of cultural developments for a future edition.

Witchcraft for Tomorrow by Doreen Valiente: If you're looking to find out more about Witchcraft, the first book I always recommend is *Witchcraft for Tomorrow* by Doreen Valiente, the mother of modern Witchcraft/Wicca. Much of the beautiful poetic language that you can find in Wicca came from Doreen, and she continued to research historical Witchcraft and folklore after parting ways with Gerald Gardner. I love her attitude and her no-nonsense approach, seasoned with a dash of whimsy. Also check out her books *Natural Magic* and *The Rebirth of Witchcraft*.

The Witch's Book of Power and *The Witch's Book of Spirits* by Devin Hunter (Woodbury, MN: Llewellyn, 2016 and 2017). If you're looking for something more recent, with a more modern take on Witchcraft, check out these two books by Devin Hunter. The latter is especially good if you'd like to read more in depth about working with spirits, deities, and other entities.

Interested in learning more about Modern Traditional Witchcraft? Visit www.moderntraditional witch.com to get started. I started the website in 1998, so it's been going a long time and was recently revamped. It also has more books for you to check out. For weekly ramblings, follow my blog at Patheos, *A Modern Traditional Witch*.

With the rising cost of print media, there are fewer hard-copy Pagan magazines on the market, but a subscription to *Witches & Pagans* magazine from BBI Media will definitely make you and your mailbox happy. You can also enjoy their online blogosphere at www.witchesandpagans.com. If you're into reading blogs, check out the wealth of Pagan voices you can feast your eyes and brain on at www.patheos.com/Pagan.

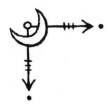

INDEX OF SYMBOLS

anchor, 28, 70, 138

arrow, 45, 47, 76, 85, 99, 138, 165, 166, 168, 170, 171, 174, 182

bowl, 162, 167, 172

butterfly, 71

chevron, 12, 19, 28, 40, 45, 47, 48, 49, 50, 53, 55, 85, 162, 173, 176-178, 182

circle, 12, 19, 40, 64, 66, 84, 125, 142, 146, 162, 163, 169, 172, 174, 176, 182

colors, 7, 10, 21, 38, 82, 116

crescent, 54, 99, 146, 162-167, 172, 173, 176, 182

    waning, 54, 182

    waxing, 54, 165, 166, 182

cross, 12, 28, 44, 46, 169, 174

diamond, 53

directions, 47, 60, 76, 99, 136, 177

dot, 7, 12, 14, 19, 23, 28, 38, 39, 40, 42, 77, 84, 85, 168, 169, 173, 174, 176, 182

    closed, 39, 40, 174

    open, 40, 168

elements, 59, 63, 75, 80, 111-114, 136, 182, 202

eye, 64, 165, 172

flower, 75, 178

hand, 9, 12, 14, 16

heart, 12, 62, 99, 162, 163, 169, 170, 174

hexagon, 57, 58, 60, 84

hourglass, 65, 170

infinity, 65, 77, 147

key/keyhole, 68

leaf, 75, 85, 165, 166, 173

letters, 3, 26, 37, 38, 81, 132, 149, 167

lines

    dashed/dotted, 42

    diagonal, 19, 41, 43, 46

    horizontal, 41, 44, 48, 52, 75, 138, 144, 165, 172, 174, 178

    vertical, 19, 41, 44, 48, 52, 61, 85, 144, 169, 173

wavy, 12, 14, 19, 21, 48, 49, 85, 167
zigzag, 12, 14, 49

mandorla, 63, 64, 85, 168, 173

numbers, 38, 77, 149

pentagon, 56, 57, 58, 171
polygons, 58

rectangle, 52

scales, 69, 99
shield, 19, 31, 53, 56, 66, 162, 169
spiral, 12, 14, 19, 21, 53, 55, 56, 57, 62, 99, 147, 162, 168, 169, 173, 177
spoon, 73
square, 51-53, 84, 136, 176
star, 12, 23, 56, 59-61, 77, 85, 138, 143-145, 165, 166, 170, 171, 174, 177, 179,
    182
    five-pointed, 56, 59, 143, 145, 182
    six-pointed, 12, 60, 77, 144, 170, 177
    seven-pointed, 145
    eight-pointed, 61

triangle, 12, 27, 28, 45, 50, 53, 60, 63, 75, 84, 144, 162, 163, 167, 170, 174,
    177

vesica piscis, 63

wheels, 66
wings, 67, 177

X, 12, 46, 61, 66, 76, 144, 174, 178

zodiac, 79, 177

To Write to the Author

If you wish to contact the author or would like more information about this book, please write to the author in care of Llewellyn Worldwide Ltd. and we will forward your request. Both the author and the publisher appreciate hearing from you and learning of your enjoyment of this book and how it has helped you. Llewellyn Worldwide Ltd. cannot guarantee that every letter written to the author can be answered, but all will be forwarded. Please write to:

Laura Tempest Zakroff
℅ Llewellyn Worldwide
2143 Wooddale Drive
Woodbury, MN 55125-2989

Please enclose a self-addressed stamped envelope for reply,
or $1.00 to cover costs. If outside the U.S.A., enclose
an international postal reply coupon.

Many of Llewellyn's authors have websites with additional information and resources.
For more information, please visit our website at www.llewellyn.com.

GET MORE AT LLEWELLYN.COM

Visit us online to browse hundreds of our books and decks, plus
sign up to receive our e-newsletters and exclusive online offers.

- **Free tarot readings • Spell-a-Day • Moon phases**
- **Recipes, spells, and tips • Blogs • Encyclopedia**
- **Author interviews, articles, and upcoming events**

GET SOCIAL WITH LLEWELLYN

Find us on  @LlewellynBooks

www.Facebook.com/LlewellynBooks

GET BOOKS AT LLEWELLYN

LLEWELLYN ORDERING INFORMATION

Order online: Visit our website at www.llewellyn.com to select your
books and place an order on our secure server.

Order by phone:
- Call toll free within the US at 1-877-NEW-WRLD (1-877-639-9753)
- We accept VISA, MasterCard, American Express, and Discover.

Order by mail:
Send the full price of your order (MN residents add 6.875% sales tax)
in US funds plus postage and handling to: Llewellyn Worldwide,
2143 Wooddale Drive, Woodbury, MN 55125-2989

POSTAGE AND HANDLING

STANDARD (US): (Please allow 12 business days)
$30.00 and under, add $6.00.
$30.01 and over, FREE SHIPPING.

CANADA:
We cannot ship to Canada. Please shop
your local bookstore or Amazon Canada.

INTERNATIONAL:
Customers pay the actual shipping cost to the final
destination, which includes tracking information.

Visit us online for more shipping options.
Prices subject to change.

FREE CATALOG!

To order, call
1-877-
NEW-WRLD
ext. 8236
or visit our
website